REINVENTING MASCULINITY

REINVENTING MASCULINITY

THE LIBERATING POWER OF COMPASSION AND CONNECTION

EDWARD M. ADAMS and ED FRAUENHEIM

Berrett–Koehler Publishers, Inc.

Berrett-Koehler Publishers, Inc.   Tel: (510) 817–2277
1333 Broadway, Suite 1000   Fax: (510) 817–2278
Oakland, CA 94612–1921   www.bkconnection.com

ORDERING INFORMATION

Quantity sales. Special discounts are available on quantity purchases by corporations, associations, and others. For details, contact the "Special Sales Department" at the Berrett-Koehler address above.

Individual sales. Berrett-Koehler publications are available through most bookstores. They can also be ordered directly from Berrett-Koehler: Tel: (800) 929–2929; Fax: (802) 864–7626; www.bkconnection.com.

Orders for college textbook/course adoption use. Please contact Berrett-Koehler: Tel: (800) 929–2929; Fax: (802) 864–7626.

Distributed to the U.S. trade and internationally by Penguin Random House Publisher Services.

Berrett-Koehler and the BK logo are registered trademarks of Berrett-Koehler Publishers, Inc.

Printed in Canada

Berrett-Koehler books are printed on long-lasting acid-free paper. When it is available, we choose paper that has been manufactured by environmentally responsible processes. These may include using trees grown in sustainable forests, incorporating recycled paper, minimizing chlorine in bleaching, or recycling the energy produced at the paper mill.

LIBRARY OF CONGRESS CATALOGING-IN-PUBLICATION DATA

Names: Adams, Edward M., author. | Frauenheim, Ed, author.
Title: Reinventing masculinity : the liberating power of compassion and connection / Edward M. Adams and Ed Frauenheim.
Description: First edition. | Oakland, CA : Berrett-Koehler Publishers, [2020] | Includes bibliographical references and index.
Identifiers: LCCN 2020016096 | ISBN 9781523088966 (paperback) | ISBN 9781523088973 (pdf) | ISBN 9781523088980 (epub)
Subjects: LCSH: Masculinity. | Men—Psychology. | Compassion.
Classification: LCC BF692.5 .A32 2020 | DDC 155.3/32—dc23
LC record available at https://lccn.loc.gov/2020016096

FIRST EDITION

26 25 24 23 22 21 20 :: 10 9 8 7 6 5 4 3 2 1

Chapter opening illustrations by Edward M. Adams; book producer and text designer: BookMatters; cover designer: Wes Youssi, M8obranding.com; copyeditor: Kirsten Janene-Nelson; proofer: Janet Reed Blake; indexer: Leonard Rosenbaum

Dr. Ed Adams: To those who understand the power of compassion and to those open to learn. And to the countless lives that have been harmed or destroyed whenever compassion is ignored.

Ed Frauenheim: To my son Julius, for teaching me how to be a better man.

CONTENTS

FOREWORD

I was delighted to be asked to write a foreword for this book by Ed Adams and Ed Frauenheim because it offers deep insights into the problematic nature of modern masculine identities.

What we become as men is so much out of our control. We didn't choose to be a male—to have the genes, bodies, and the early life social conditioning we have. Males often engage in aggressive competition with other males for reproductive opportunities. Females too create their own hierarchies. We find our social competition culturally textured. We find ourselves with impulses, attitudes, and beliefs about the way we should be.

For men, this is typically some archetypal version of a "hero" prepared to sacrifice life and limb for kin and country, for honor and tribute. We are to be tough and fearless: to hide emotions of fear, grief, vulnerability, and despair, to be the right stuff. We live in fear of being shamed as a wimp or a coward, as unwanted or irrelevant![1] As so much entertainment infecting young males demonstrates—from James Bond myths to Superman and the Avengers—it's all about power to defeat the other.

This book highlights the fact that it doesn't have to be

like that. Indeed, new evidence suggests that during the few million years we evolved into hunter-gatherers, males were relatively nonaggressive; their status was gained through altruism, caring, and sharing—and sexuality was open. Our basic nature has been deeply corrupted. Modern cultures have basically driven us all crazy.[2]

Yet we're also beginning to understand the evolution of emotional needs and what brings out the best and worst in us. With such insights, many of which are expertly outlined in this book, we can gain new awareness about who we are and what we can become. We can consider if the roles we inherited are good for us, for our relationships, and indeed for humanity. The reality is they are not, and they haven't been for many thousands of years.[3]

Modern anthropologists are finding that early humans were not particularly aggressive. Instead, scholars are pointing to very peace-loving and caring human beings in the hunter-gatherer groups that were the primary social structure that shaped our minds. In fact, it's likely that human intelligence and language evolved partly *because* we focused on developing prosocial relationships.[4] This isn't to romanticize hunter-gatherers, because some were and are quite aggressive. Yet, we also know that when social environments are benign then male psychology is also benign.[5]

If we are by nature quite benign, peace-loving, and caring, then where did it all go wrong? Most scholars point to one thing: agriculture. With agriculture the hunter-gatherer way of life gradually disappeared. Then, as groups got larger, static settlements emerged, and resources expanded. This opened the way for aggressive dominant males to race to the top of the hierarchy, threatening all those below them.[6]

And where has this got us? It's tragic to consider the billions of men who have rushed at each other with spears and swords, the guns and bombs that over the centuries have left screaming, terrified, and dying bodies strewn over countless battlefields. Why are men so vicious toward other human beings? Why do we spend so much of our energy inventing sharper blades, longer-flying arrows, and more-powerful bombs to kill and maim? We must face the fact that we are a species with extreme potentials: both to inflict great harm and to offer profound compassion.

The message in this book will help wake us up. And it may make us angry. That anger comes from becoming aware that we men have been scripted to see ourselves as nothing but disposable bits of DNA, strutting our stuff, prepared to step on whoever gets in our way—and to be stepped on. This can be seen on countless battlefields, on the football field, and in our race to the top of million-dollar salaries. It suits one group only, and that's the ruling elite.

How can we free ourselves from this absurd, competitive, destructive, and intensely hierarchical culture? First, we must begin to care for each other. We have to start to care about being men connected with the destiny of other men. Men all over the world need to say "enough is enough." We need to demand better social conditions and wiser scripts for us all. We need to demand better entertainment, better education, better emotional support, better guidance, and better leadership.

Women too have had an incredibly bad deal in the last five to ten thousand years as a result of male hierarchies. Females have been exploited, traded and raped, suppressed and marginalized, and even in religion treated as second class. But they are rebelling more and more, and quite rightly too.

Men can support that. And we should do so without hanging our heads in shame. We must see the tragedies we've all gotten caught in as coming from gene-built and culturally shaped scripts that none of us chose. We did not choose our brains or social environments. But we must aspire to be compassion-focused and live our lives as helpfully as we can.

As this book's authors highlight, men need to reclaim compassionate courage as a basic human trait that we can craft our identities around—one that offers meaning and purpose, dignity and wisdom. This is necessary if we are to stop the way our societies pit us against each other. We must stop falling for the idea that hostile competition is somehow heroic while denying that it's also deeply harmful. With a proper understanding of what compassion actually is, and what happens in our brains when we practice and enact it, we begin to see that it is the root of well-being. It is not submissive but assertive. It insists on equality and fairness. It insists on creating a world that we all want to live in and enjoy.

Reinventing Masculinity is a wonderful book for thinking about how to release ourselves from crippling processes. It's time for us all to stand up and say, "Give us back our full humanity; give us back our dignity." Let us find our courage, so that when it's our time to die we know we've tried to make the world a better, less competitive, more caring place.

Paul Gilbert
PhD, OBE, Professor of Clinical Psychology at the University of Derby, founder of compassion-focused therapy and author of several books, including *The Compassionate Mind: A New Approach to Life's Challenges* and *Living Like Crazy*

PREFACE

This book is an act of hope and love. We believe men matter, and matter a lot. While this might seem obvious, it's important to examine and update how our culture directs men to develop and mature, cultivate loving relationships, express intimacy, succeed at work, and contribute to our communities. These actions touch everyone and everything that exists.

In other words, how we define masculinity is a fundamental element of our cultural life. We wrote this book to take a good look at the models of masculinity that consciously and unconsciously—often invisibly—influence all of us.

We found both bad and good news. First the bad news: the approach to manhood that dominates our culture is unhealthy, outdated, and dangerous.

The good news is that men are reinventing masculinity—or aspire to reinvent masculinity—in ways that make sense for our times, enable men to thrive, and offer hope for a better future for all of us.

This book is an attempt to support the shift from a confined masculinity to one that is liberating. To a masculinity that frees both men and women from oppressive limitations and to live more expansive, compassionate, and connected lives.

Two Eds Are Better Than One

The two of us came together to tell this story in a way neither of us could do on our own. Here's what we each brought to the project.

DR. ED ADAMS is a licensed psychologist in private practice. He is also past president of the Society for the Psychological Study of Men and Masculinities, also known as Division 51 of the American Psychological Association (APA). In 2015, this division awarded Ed the Practitioner of the Year Award. For over thirty years, Ed has treated men in individual and group therapy. In 1990, Ed founded Men Mentoring Men (M3), a nonprofit organization in New Jersey designed to help men live larger and more meaningful lives as expressions of the "best of masculinity." Ed has facilitated growth in many men from the inside out through thousands of psychotherapy sessions, men's group meetings, and retreats.

Ed's experience as a psychologist and men's group leader has made him no stranger to the joys and sorrows men often experience but seldom share. Moreover, his personal experiences as a boy and man, including coping with a loving yet alcoholic father suffering from PTSD after long service in World War II, heightened his sensitivity to the complexity and challenges of the male experience. These experiences—of being a husband to a loving and supportive wife, of being a proud father of a thoughtful and caring son—have humbled, educated, and strengthened him. Ed's personal and professional life experiences have fortified his commitment to share what he has learned through this book.

Ed also has been at the center of a masculinity firestorm in the media. As past president of Division 51, Ed was one of the spokesmen for the APA's new guidelines for treating men and boys. These guidelines were the product of four decades of research. Yet they immediately sparked controversy in the media when they were made public in early 2019. Conservative commentators blasted the research, which found that rigid adherence to traditional masculinity traits like aggression, dominance, and stoicism tend to be unhealthy—for men as well as for those in their lives. Ed explained the meaning of the guidelines on the *Good Morning America* TV show with host Michael Strahan. He also appeared on NPR, as well as on conservative pundit Laura Ingraham's Fox News program, among many other media appearances.[1]

Ed Adams is also a professional artist—painter, sculptor, and poet—who for twenty-five years owned an art gallery showcasing his paintings and sculptures. Two of Ed's public sculptures honor ordinary men who during the Second World War showed extraordinary courage, connection, and compassion. Ed's monumental sculpture in Smith Field Park in Parsippany, New Jersey, honors Raoul Wallenberg, who is credited with saving over 100,000 lives. And Ed's bust of Oskar Schindler, who prevented the certain death of 1,200 Jews, now occupies a place of honor in the office of Steven Spielberg, director of the movie *Schindler's List*. Both Wallenberg and Schindler were men who exemplified the best of masculinity while thrust amid the worst of humanity.

Since we feel this book should reflect the diversity and full-ness of the masculinity we espouse, Ed's paintings, vignettes, and poetry are integrated into the content of this book.

ED FRAUENHEIM is an author who has written about busi-ness, leadership, and society for more than two decades. Ed currently serves as senior director of content at Great Place to Work, the research and advisory company best known for producing the annual *Fortune* 100 Best Companies to Work for in America list. Ed also cofounded the Teal Team, a small organization dedicated to helping organizations evolve into more democratic, purpose-driven, soulful places.

Before these roles, Ed spent twenty years as a journalist and commentator focused on the intersection of work, technol-ogy, and business strategy. He has cowritten three books, in-cluding *A Great Place to Work for All: Better for Business, Better for People, Better for the World*.[2] That 2018 book included Great Place to Work's research on 10,000 managers and 75,000 em-ployees. Ed and his coauthors discovered that the most inclu-sive and effective leaders—dubbed "For All Leaders"—have traits such as humility, curiosity, a focus on purpose, and the ability to cultivate trusting relationships.

Through that research and other articles and reports, Ed's work has explored the way our more complex, interconnected economy and global society are calling on men to break free of the narrow version of masculinity most of us grew up with. While a culture war rages in the mass media over what it means to be a man, Ed has contributed to a quieter though nonetheless vibrant conversation in the world of work and organizations. He has observed a growing consensus in the business world: it no longer works to be autocratic, cutthroat, or emotionally unavailable. Ed has sought to connect the dots, to bridge these conversations to show that a different masculinity works at work today.

Ed Frauenheim also brings a lifelong struggle with "man-rules" to this book. Be strong? Ed grew up skinny. Dominate others? He lost his one fist fight in sixth grade. Just win, baby? He often froze during key moments of hockey, basketball, and soccer games.[3] The traditional male obsessions with winning, with brute strength, with becoming king of the corporate hill have haunted Ed for much of his life. But through personal reflection, mindful practices, and plenty of help, he has come to redefine traits like emotional sensitivity, exuberance, and camaraderie as worthy. He is living a fuller life as a result, and feels like a better husband to his wife and father to his son and daughter.

Who Should Read This Book?

We wrote *Reinventing Masculinity* with several audiences in mind. The first is individual men seeking guidance on becoming a better man and living a better life. We imagine women seeking to better understand men's needs will find the book valuable as well. It should also prove useful to mental health professionals and therapists treating men in individual and couples counseling. We also expect it will serve teachers and coaches—whether they be athletic, life, or business coaches.

We wrote *Reinventing Masculinity* with organizations in mind as well. We believe it can help business leaders cultivate more effective, inclusive, and soulful cultures. In a similar vein, we are hopeful the book will contribute insights to academic courses in fields ranging from gender studies to psychology to management.

Finally, we believe the book will be useful and inspiring to men's groups akin to Ed Adams's M3 groups as well as therapy or treatment groups. To help groups get the most out of reading the book together, we've included a Discussion Guide at the end of the book.

We also created a Reinventing Masculinity Self-Assessment—you will find it after the Discussion Guide. By answering the assessment's ten questions, any man can get a rough sense of where he sits on a continuum. On one extreme is what we call "confined masculinity," and on the other is "liberating masculinity." This tool is designed to help men locate where they are in their journey toward a freer, bigger, better life.

Gender Bending and Mending

We are hopeful that our book will be meaningful to the majority of men. That's because the up-to-now dominant, confined masculinity we describe has influence over all men, regardless of how they define their identities or practice their sexuality. Still, we want to acknowledge that our message is directed primarily to a particular audience. We are speaking for the most part about, and to, heterosexual men. In addition, the cramped masculinity we describe in the book tends to be felt most acutely by men who came of age in the twentieth century—Baby Boomers, members of Generation X, and older Millennials. What's more, our stories and suggestions are geared toward "cisgender" men. That is, men who identify with the gender of their biological sex—as male rather than as female or nonbinary.

The very terms "cisgender" and "nonbinary" may be unfamiliar and even disturbing to many men who grew up with constrained views regarding the identities available to human beings. Those constrained views are at the heart of this book. As authors, we hope to help mend wounds that have resulted from fearful, intolerant ideas about gender roles—by which we mean the many social and cultural ways people of either sex express themselves. Not only do we honor the diversity of gender identities, we also appreciate the way masculinity is flavored by a variety of factors, including race, national origin, socio-economic status, and religion.

We'd like to add that—as two white, middle-class, middle-aged, heterosexual American men—we know our ability to comprehend the experiences of the entirety of men, not to mention women, is imperfect. But at the same time, we believe there is value in the two of us drawing from our experience, our expertise, and our empathy to share what we've learned. We've come to know a lot about stereotypic masculinity, and we see signs that even younger men and people who are adopting alternative genders find themselves damaged by that traditional, still-potent masculine ideology.

We hope this book highlights the ways that central beliefs about masculinity have shaped people's lives, how those core assumptions are hurting us, and how a better, liberating version of manhood is emerging. What's more, we see this reinvented masculinity as being built on universal principles. Compassion and connection are fundamental human attributes. As we see it, all people—and all living creatures—will benefit when we embrace those virtues.

High Stakes and Active Imaginations

Our intention is to advance and contribute to public and personal narratives about men and masculinity. We want to "stir the pot," to critically examine the expectations we place on boys and men, as well as to offer expanded possibilities and alternatives. We do this because the stakes are high. We see the reinvention of masculinity as crucial to the fate of life itself. This was clearly demonstrated by the COVID-19 pandemic that swept across the globe just as we completed our book manuscript. The worldwide crisis left no doubt that humanity's physical and emotional health depends upon a recognition of our interwoven connections, as well as our ability to demonstrate self-compassion and compassion for others.

To put it bluntly: disconnected and non-compassionate men who espouse hate, shame, and violence are toxic. Men who are indifferent, lazy, and easily swayed by mean-spirited ideas can be downright dangerous. And men unwilling to cooperate or solve problems *together* stand in the way of progress. We believe the cramped, antiquated model of masculinity that leads to toxic, dangerous, and inflexible behavior must be challenged by the majority of men who live caring, loving, and productive lives. We can no longer be silent, we can no longer expect women to carry our emotional burdens, and we can no longer assume that good conquers evil.

We intend this book to offer positive alternatives to the male toolbox. We also ask both men and women to enter this dialogue. It's clear that no real change in our ideas of manhood can occur or be sustained without the support of women. Men and women need only one goal in common to motivate cooperation between us—the desire to create a kinder, more harmonious, more socially just, and peaceful world. True peace begins within every individual's heart and mind. We're talking about cooperation between the sexes that leads to such a peace, rather than a mere cease fire.

From our different experiences and paths, the two of us Eds have arrived at the same conclusion. A masculinity adapted to the times in which we live requires two things above all else: first, that compassion become a prized masculine trait; and second, that men rediscover connections with all of life. We will illustrate these themes throughout the book with examples and anecdotes. All the stories are fundamentally true. In many cases, the stories include people's actual names. Other times, we have changed names and altered some details to protect people's identities.

Finally, a word about imagination. If we couldn't imagine flying in the air like a migrating bird, manned flight would not be possible. All of the engineering, trials and errors and hours of focused work built the first airplane. But that was possible, first and foremost, because it existed in imagination.

This book provides practical information for breaking free from an obsolete way of being a man and for moving to a healthier, powerful, and expansive masculinity. But the book will be most effective when you engage your imagination— when you consider how masculinity can be reinvented in your personal life, in your place of work, in your community, and in our world. Thank you for imagining along with us.

A New Day

INTRODUCTION
Reinventing Masculinity

"I hope to figure out why I am so unhappy."

These were the words spoken by John as he began a counseling session with coauthor Ed Adams.

The two talked further, and John rounded up the usual suspects of a less-than-satisfying life. He spoke about his work. Despite having risen through the corporate ranks to a high-paying position, John felt insecure about his job performance. He said his marriage was "going stale." And that he'd turned to other women for pleasure and company. He also mentioned that he had no "close" friends and frequently felt alone.

John often drank to ease all those pains. Still, he was insightful, thoughtful, and articulate—and seemed very motivated to find more fulfillment.

What was at the root of his unhappiness?

We believe it had much to do with narrow beliefs about what it means to be a man.

John didn't make this connection between his problems and male gender roles. Nor do many men who experience similar feelings of loneliness and, what's more, the fear of being discovered as not "enough" of a man.

But the truth is that John and a multitude of other men are caught in the grip of what we call "confined masculinity." Confined masculinity is a cramped, outdated, and increasingly dangerous version of manhood. It limits and hurts men as individuals—in our family and friend circles, in our organizations, and in our global society. In fact, we go so far as to say the fate of the human race could hinge on the ability of men and women to reimagine gender roles better suited for the twenty-first century. If so, then it's up to men to reimagine masculine ideology.

The stakes are high—but the news is good. Men across the globe are bravely redefining masculinity, breaking free of obsolete expectations and embracing an expansive, compassionate, connected, soulful manhood that works for all. But before we learn more about those pioneers, let's map the traditional male territory they are moving beyond. Let's outline confined masculinity.

Confined Masculinity

"Confined masculinity" refers to a set of attitudes, values, and behaviors that define how men "should" show up in the world. It is a constrained conception of masculinity, one in which men tend to define themselves as playing just a few dominant roles—the protector, the provider, and the conqueror. The "confined" nature of this masculinity also applies to *how, where,* and *for whom* they play these roles. "Confined men" almost exclusively see themselves as being in competition with others. They believe they need to demonstrate physical courage and project confidence—however false. They also concentrate attention on exterior markers—such as physical strength, financial success, and social status. Less attention is paid to interior matters, like emotion and spirit. As for the "for whom" portion of this, confined men tend to restrict their efforts as protectors, providers, and conquerors to serve a relatively tight circle: themselves, their immediate families, and a limited number of others.

Confined masculinity focuses on a man's separateness more than on his sense of belonging. For example, many confined men believe they should keep emotions to themselves, be self-sufficient, and show no vulnerability. Confined masculinity also has a fundamentally fearful outlook, a mindset of scarcity and ever-present danger. Confined masculinity effectively puts men in a defensive crouch, ready to snarl at perceived threats, predisposed to lash out and stuck with a distorted view of their surroundings

The tendency toward isolation and suspicion leads men, on the one hand, to become self-absorbed. Yet it also conditions them to band together against people defined as "other"— creating racial, religious, or economic divides—and at times explode with anger, aggression, and even violence.

Confined men are often hyper-competitive. Many demean women and people who don't fit standard sexual norms. Their sense of self-worth tends to depend on their victories—which often come at the expense of others.

Confined masculinity maps to rigid, traditional notions of what a "real" man is supposed to be: the stoic warrior and patriarch. This conception of manhood has dominated much of human culture for several thousand years. But, as we will see later in the book, that concept is neither preordained nor biologically determined. Gender roles—the ways people of different sexes express their identities—have proven to be remarkably fluid across the history of our species. They have changed in response to a variety of factors, including shifts in our economy, our beliefs, and our culture.

Confined Masculinity and the Twenty-First Century

Gender roles are changing again today. The shifts underway have much to do with the shortcomings of confined masculinity that are becoming ever-more apparent. The confined male code of behavior isn't just insufficient for men's success individually or collectively, it's also measurably harmful. It isn't a masculinity that works for the twenty-first century.

Most men get this. In a 2018 poll conducted by media organization FiveThirtyEight, 60 percent of men surveyed said society puts pressure on men to behave in a way that is unhealthy or bad.[1] Indeed, ample evidence now demonstrates that confined masculinity contributes to depression, suicide, and violence in men.[2] Men account for 78 percent of suicides in the United States and three in ten American men have suffered from depression.[3]

In effect, a confined masculinity limits a man's ability to live a large, full life. Both the compressed definition and truncated expression of men's roles make it hard for a man to integrate foundational aspects of his own humanity, including his need to belong and his instinct to care for others. Confined masculinity shrinks his imagination of himself and others—while also curbing his ability both to have healthy relationships with family members and to develop and maintain meaningful friendships.

Similarly, confined masculinity no longer works at work. Most companies feature hierarchical structures and impersonal practices that mimic traditional masculine values. But this approach is proving to be incompatible with our increasingly complex, globally integrated economy and with growing attention to the well-being of people and planet. Stressful, toxic workplaces contribute to some 120,000 premature deaths a year, and the average company operates at just a fraction of its potential to innovate and grow.[4] More and more companies have been recognizing these problems. And they have been changing in ways that challenge confined men. Organizations increasingly expect leaders and other employees to demonstrate traits like empathy, curiosity, and collaboration. These are nearly the opposite characteristics of a confined masculinity.

Finally, a confined male consciousness—with its truncated imagination and myopic perspective along with its embrace of hyper-individualism, pecking orders, and physical aggression—is fueling some of the biggest problems we face today as a global society. These include deepening economic inequality and insecurity, racism and the rise of violent white nationalism, objectification and abuse of women, and homophobia.[5] Confined masculinity's failure to view the world in a systemic way interferes with our ability to anticipate and respond to pandemics and other large-scale health issues. What's more, this limited male ethos contributes to what is arguably the greatest peril confronting humanity: the global climate crisis.

In fact, many confined men deny that climate change is real, much less a threat.

To be sure, confined masculinity has benefited some men a great deal and has fueled many achievements in human history. But it has also treated many men as disposable weapons and worker ants, sending them off to war and soul-killing workplaces and depriving them of their dignity and value as *whole* human beings. Altogether, the confined male ethos has trapped us in self-destructive patterns that threaten the survival of life on earth.

What is required is a reinvention and a reimaging of masculinity. We need a masculinity that reframes traditional masculine traits such as strength, valor, and courage. We need a masculinity that applies virtuous values more universally, and that incorporates an elevated consciousness about the interconnectedness of all people, of all life. This is a shift in consciousness from an orientation of "me" to one of "me and we"—a perspective that acknowledges the importance of others in our thoughts, words, and deeds.

That is, we need a masculinity that includes worthy elements of the past while also stretching beyond old limits to meet our new realities. The realities of the twenty-first century include the rise of sexual and racial justice, the movement to create parity in all facets of life. Humanity also faces increased complexity in arenas ranging from technology to commerce to society. What's more, we confront a heightened risk of planetary disaster—be that a deadly pandemic, nuclear conflict, or climate catastrophe.

What's needed, in other words, is a masculinity that is comfortable with and respectful of more assertive and autonomous women. A masculinity comfortable with men expressing tenderness and care—qualities that have long been labeled "feminine" but that actually are deeply human. A masculinity capable of both seeing a wider societal perspective and acquiring the skills to comprehend and navigate today's complexity. A masculinity willing to recognize the interconnections of all people and cultures as well as our environment. A masculinity willing to engage with global problems with urgency, compassion, and creativity.

Enter Liberating Masculinity

Thankfully, such a manhood is emerging. On the opposite end of the spectrum from confined masculinity is what we call "liberating masculinity." With "liberating" we refer to two meanings. The first is the sense that men are freed to live bigger, fuller, more imaginative lives. The second is that this is a masculinity that involves freeing others. As such, it is an emancipation that works both inwardly and outwardly. It is about freedom for an individual man as well as that man liberating others.

Liberating masculinity is a version of masculinity that releases men from the limiting, damaging, counterproductive bonds of traditional views of manhood. It enables men to embody many archetypal roles, extending beyond the conventional provider and protector roles to others such as healer, artist, lover, and spiritual seeker. A man operating from liberating masculinity also has a broader understanding of how to perform his multiple roles.

For example, he sees himself as a defender of psychological

safety in his home and work settings. He takes a stand against the bullying and humiliations that damage both kids and colleagues, knowing that emotional harm can scar families as well as lower the bottom line for businesses. A man embracing liberating masculinity does not view himself as the center of things, but rather as part of the whole. He cares about all human beings and all life on earth.

Liberating masculinity includes valor, strength, and achievement—some of the same aspects celebrated in the traditional view of masculinity. But in a reinvented, liberating masculinity, these traits are transformed. Instead of the self-absorption found in confined masculinity, a liberating man recognizes the impact of his actions or inactions on others. He therefore applies his courage, might, and perseverance in service to others. In this way, liberating masculinity is a virtuous masculinity.

Liberating masculinity manages fear differently than confined masculinity does. The liberating man doesn't deny or run from fears but moves toward them. He develops the ability to self-regulate anxiety, anger, and other emotions. While a confined man crouches fearfully, the liberating man stands tall and spreads his arms wide. He is unafraid to embrace life and capable of seeing the world around him clearly.

The liberating man has fears, including self-doubt. And he is not naïve—but neither is he fear-driven. Instead, he demonstrates the courage to deal with reality just as it is, and he approaches the world with a mindset of abundance and appreciation. He possesses a fundamental acceptance of both his imperfect self and the foibles of others. He accepts the joys and disappointments of life without rigid attachment to either one.

A deep sense of trust informs another key feature of liberating masculinity. If confined masculinity tends to cultivate close-minded fighters, liberating masculinity produces open-hearted friends. The liberating man prioritizes harmonious relationships by choosing to live in peace with other peoples and with nature.

Compassion and Connection

This focus on relationships is seen in two key ingredients of liberating masculinity: compassion and connection. The compassion element begins with self-compassion, with the ability and willingness to acknowledge, accept, and experience emotions like sadness, anger, joy, disappointment, guilt, and wonder. Men tend to be very hard on themselves, and often judge themselves harshly when they think they're not living up to social conceptions of who they should be. A lack of self-compassion leads to feelings of shame—which in turn make it harder for men to demonstrate compassion for others. But self-compassion inspires men to address their own suffering, such as by making difficult-but-necessary decisions, asking for help, and forgiving themselves when they make mistakes.

"Compassion" means, literally, to feel with others. To experience the distress of another and act to alleviate or end that distress. Through compassion, the liberating man helps himself and others find purpose, peace, and genuine satisfaction.

Compassion toward others is closely linked to forming connections with others, and to understanding our interdependence. Connection takes many forms. It can range from intimate romantic love to devoted fathering to deep "philia" or brotherly love. It can be expressed by participating in an organized cause or in local, state, and federal governance. Connection recognizes our common humanity with peoples across the globe and a sense of unity with and responsibility to all life.

Perhaps this description of a liberating masculinity seems like a moonshot—an idealistic image of manhood that could never take root in the hearts of men.

But liberating masculinity *is* taking root. Men, and women, all around the world are participating in a quiet and often private revolution concerning masculinity. You're likely one of them.

Most men know something is wrong with many of the rules we've absorbed since childhood. And men today are rewriting the rules of manhood. Not surprisingly, many of the masculinity rebels are young. They include David Hogg, one of the survivors of the Parkland, Florida, high school shooting massacre, who has continued to speak out against gun violence. Other men breaking the man-mold are older, prominent, public leaders in various fields. Men like Steve Kerr, who coached the Golden State Warriors professional basketball team to several championships based on values that included mindfulness, compassion, and joy. Or Chuck Robbins, CEO of giant technology company Cisco Systems, who was inspired by a dream to tap his organization's significant resources to help solve the problem of homelessness. (We'll say more about these last two later on.)

Many others moving toward a liberating masculinity are everyday men living everyday lives. They are questioning confined masculinity, uncomfortable with its combative ethos, aware of its increasing ineffectiveness, or suffering from its strictures. They are men like John, with whom we began this chapter. Depressed and hurting, he opened up in his therapy sessions. John admitted he felt vulnerable in doing so. But he said that therapy would only be helpful if he took a risk and "let my truth out."

And he went further. He agreed to participate in a men's group Ed Adams founded, Men Mentoring Men (M3). M3 is a male-friendly not-for-profit organization designed for men to gather and discuss life. M3 has one rule: "no man shames another." In M3 meetings, John discovered that many of the feelings that he'd assumed were abnormal—his work anxiety, his loneliness, his sense that his marriage was a failure, even his need for love—were far from unusual. Other men described the same or similar emotions. John not only found reassurance in the stories of other men, he also found himself supporting and mentoring peers within his group.

John's decision to seek counseling and join a men's group represented an act of courage. It represented defiance of the traditional views that see weakness in acknowledging emotional pain, seeking help, and comforting others. Such views are off-base and obsolete. In the world that is emerging, the qualities of compassion and self-compassion, of empathy and connection, are proving to be freeing, powerful, and necessary.

The Liberating Power of Compassion and Connection

Consider the effect of a liberating masculinity on Jerry, another of Ed Adam's former patients. For decades, Jerry worked for a large insurance firm and defined himself primarily as a breadwinner for his family. He hung out with the guys at work, but the relationships were superficial and steered clear of "heavy" topics. When work stresses—including pressure to cut corners—piled up, Jerry reached a breaking point. That's when he sought counseling with Ed.

"I realized I had no interior life," Jerry says in retrospect. He hadn't realized how restricted his existence was as a typical "company man."

Jerry stuck with his therapy sessions and began participating in M3. Gradually, he shed the shackles of confined masculinity. He came to see that he needed to leave his harmful workplace and follow his own path—by becoming a personal fitness trainer. Today, at age eighty, he is going strong as a personal trainer. He's also among the leaders of M3, and one of the staunchest advocates of shattering the cage created by the rules of confined masculinity.

"I struggled to leave the security of that job, but now I'm convinced that doing so saved my life," Jerry says. "Along the way, I deepened my relationship with my wife and kids. I may not be as dollar rich as I would be if I stayed at it longer, but I sure feel wealthy."

Jerry demonstrates how liberating men are free to live richer, fuller lives. His story shows the way men can enjoy healthier, stronger bonds with their spouses, children, and friends once they move toward an expanding version of manhood. Of course, liberating masculinity doesn't erase challenges in a man's life and social circles. But it does equip him with more tools, a bigger perspective, and a greater desire to create harmony in his personal relationships. He is more capable of integrating work, love, and play—and experiences greater satisfaction as a result. So not only is a liberating man more emotionally intelligent, his view of himself and others becomes an expanding universe of possibilities.

Liberating masculinity also applies to organizations, institutions, and beyond. Many companies are beginning to understand the pitfalls of maintaining a business model that mirrors confined masculinity. Alternatives to a top-down command structure are needed in a globally interconnected, fast-paced, volatile environment. "Soft skills" like cooperation, communication, and empathy, as well as generosity itself, are surfacing as critical to success. So is curiosity. Learning and growing are vital and require vulnerability. They require the courage to admit not knowing all the answers, as well as a willingness to wonder and ask essential questions. Men who are cold, rigid, and isolated—that is to say, confined men— are less and less effective in organizations that are calling for warmth, flexibility, and connection.

A liberating masculinity also enables men to help solve the pressing problems confronting our communities and our planet. Unfettered by selfish, clannish, and myopic views, the liberating man applies a global perspective when considering challenges such as racial animosity, war, poverty, and the climate crisis. He can see other perspectives and propose creative solutions to generate a healthier, kinder, and more peaceful and prosperous world.

The Five Cs

Compassion and connection are central to liberating masculinity. They also are part of a larger recipe for reinventing masculinity. How do you move from a confined to a liberating masculinity? We believe there are five crucial ingredients, or practices, that we call the Five Cs: curiosity, courage, compassion, connection, and commitment.

Here's what we mean by each "C."

▶ CURIOSITY is asking questions and wondering—especially about whether there's more to life, and if there's a better way than the traditional, confined man-rules allow.

▶ COURAGE is challenging the subjective fears and social constraints that prevent us from expressing our multiple dimensions as men.

▶ COMPASSION is opening ourselves to the suffering and disappointment within ourselves and others.

▶ CONNECTION is noticing the interdependence of living systems and cultivating healthier bonds with people and the planet.

▶ COMMITMENT is persisting in the work to expand gender roles in favor of a liberating, powerful masculinity that works for all.

The Five Cs reflect the fact that there are multiple entry points for a man to begin reinventing his masculinity. A confined man, for example, may find his heart is touched by the story of someone's suffering, and decide that equating tenderness with weakness makes little sense. That incident could prompt him to feel greater connection—as well as newfound courage to face down fears associated with confined masculinity, including anxiety around appearing "feminine," "inadequate," or not "man enough." Imagine how that changed perspective could improve his relationships.

As this example suggests, the Five Cs interact with each other. They also are recurring and cyclical. Men reinventing their masculinity will continue to improve these five practices. Liberating masculinity means moving through all Five Cs again and again, developing an ever-freer, ever-more expansive, ever-more virtuous male ethos.

A Conscious, Soulful Reinvention of Masculinity

Even as a reinvented masculinity is about deepening the Five Cs, it reflects a higher consciousness. Liberating masculinity represents a way of thinking about the world often called a "systemic" or "integral" mindset.[6] Confined masculinity limits the ability to see the interconnections among human beings. Confined men tend to think in binary ways, as though a strong warrior couldn't also be a vulnerable lover, or as if a member of a particular country doesn't also belong to the whole human race.

Liberating masculinity reflects an elevated consciousness that enables a wider worldview. It can effectively navigate greater complexity in our organizations and society. It doesn't get boxed in by black-and-white choices. By seeing more shades of gray—while retaining a moral compass—liberating masculinity enables greater creativity and innovative problem solving.

A higher consciousness helps men in down-to-earth dilemmas, both at work and at home. It also allows men to be comfortable with matters of spirit and soul. Confined men often reject or fumble around nonvisible realities—things like love, tenderness, and spiritual or mystical truths. These kinds of realities constitute the poetry of life and account for much of the joy and deeper meaning we seek. Liberating men acknowledge, accept, and embrace these mysteries. Liberating masculinity opens the door to a healing of the soul.

Many men and women will dismiss talk of a more soulful masculinity. In general, there is great resistance today to a liberating, expansive version of manhood. Much of that resistance reflects a simplistic and unexamined attitude—a refusal to mature our masculinity.

In effect, we're in a period of great confusion and gender chaos. Even as growing numbers of people are expanding traditional gender definitions to include transgender or nonbinary identities, other men and women are doubling down on conventional stereotypes and demanding conformity. Many others are puzzled about the emerging, more complicated gender landscape. But it just may be that the confusion and turmoil are necessary to usher in a new paradigm or mythos about men and masculinity.

The fierce attacks on a liberating masculinity are nonetheless painful—for the men taking initial, cautious, and sometimes bold steps in that direction; for advocates of the transition; for our society as a whole. Consider them growing pains, part of a broader process in which human beings are moving from an adolescent consciousness to a more advanced one.

Reading *Reinventing Masculinity*

We intend this book to be both a guide for minimizing those growing pains and a map for the reinvention of masculinity. We believe it can serve individual men who are struggling to make sense of how to be a good man, spouse, and father. We want all men—and women—regardless of sexual orientation, race, education, or economic status to experience a liberating life. At the same time, we believe the book can aid business leaders as they try to help their organizations thrive by helping employees—especially male employees—become more authentic, inclusive, and effective. We also hope *Reinventing Masculinity* brings a focus to global debates about how men can show up in the world—and that it creates greater consciousness in elected officials, community leaders, and men and women across the globe.

We believe this book is best read from beginning to end. But you are invited to jump to the chapters that pique your interest immediately. The first two chapters describe confined masculinity and liberating masculinity. Chapter three examines the Five Cs in detail. The next two chapters explore the liberating power of compassion and connection in particular. Chapter six dives into how masculinity is being reinvented at work, and chapter seven explores the role of soul in liberating masculinity. We conclude by encouraging men and women to reimagine gender roles and join the movement to reinvent masculinity.

At the close of most chapters we provide practice exercises. Building on the Five Cs, these activities are designed to help men move toward liberating masculinity.

John, Reinvented

John is among the men committed to a liberating masculinity. As you may recall, John was unhappy but eager to change.

John's solution to a listless, limited life was to seek counsel, explore and identify his emotions, develop a meaningful support system, and find the courage to make difficult course corrections.

He stopped drinking and began attending Alcoholics Anonymous meetings. He also weaned himself off the frequent sexual trysts that he eventually found to be a hollow fix rather than a source of lasting fulfillment. He reached out and rediscovered a male friendship that he had "allowed to disappear." And he became a member of M3, regularly attending twice-monthly gatherings of about a dozen men.

Put simply, John worked to break free of old habits and extend himself. He became at once more introspective and more connected to others beyond himself. And as his life began to feel bigger, his work productivity grew while his job stresses shrank.

In his conversations with Ed Adams, John talked about how he'd come to see these internal and external expansions as vital to sustainable, deep satisfaction. Ed suggested a mantra for these efforts: "protect happy." This idea represented a very different kind of "protecting" than John had been familiar with—simply keeping himself and his wife physically and financially safe. That confined identity hadn't required much of him. But it had led to stagnation and sorrow.

"It's miserable but easy to be depressed," John told Ed. "Now, I can't imagine not protecting happy."

This is not to say John lived happily ever after. Not long after he joined M3, John and his wife split up. Their relationship had withered beyond repair, and John suffered during and after the divorce.

A Fable of Three Men:
Three Ways to Live Out a Liberating Masculinity

Three boys were born and raised in the same country village. And because the boys received an abundance of love, guidance, and support, they grew up to become strong and wise men.

The first man applied his strength and wisdom to acquire great wealth. He used his riches to support projects that benefited the entire village.

The second man became a highly respected leader. He applied his strength and wisdom to govern an entire region known for its long-lasting peace and tranquility.

The third man lived a simple and humble life. He applied his courage and love to cultivate his compassion and expand his imagination to include all sentient beings. His life transformed worlds.

—E. M. ADAMS

Yet he didn't suffer alone.

The friendship he'd rekindled and the men of M3 provided realistic support that boosted his spirits.

And as painful as that episode was, John had no regrets with his path overall. He was glad to have begun the lifelong process of shedding the shell of a confined masculinity. He was glad to have reinvented his understanding of manhood. And glad to have chosen a liberating masculinity—one that freed him to feel more alive.

"I figure everything that happened had to happen the way

it did," he said. "Because now I am very grateful for how my life is unfolding."

THINGS TO PONDER AND DO

CURIOSITY: Have you felt constrained by traditional notions of manhood? If so, how? Are you open to shifting your beliefs and behaviors as a man? Why or why not?

COURAGE: Look in a mirror and talk to yourself about ways you may have harmed yourself or others based on confined views of masculinity.

COMPASSION: Can you say kind words to a man you know who may be stuck in fear or destructive patterns?

CONNECTION: Can you initiate a conversation or exchange with someone in your personal life or work to build a deeper relationship with them than you've had up to now?

COMMITMENT: What is a change in your daily routine that would breathe life into your masculine soul? Can you commit to making that change for a week?

Locked Inside

1 Outdated and Unhealthy: Confined Masculinity

For a good example of a man stuck in confined masculinity, meet Ben.

Ben was a patient of coauthor Ed Adams several years ago.

Ben began his first session of therapy with a grin and a self-assured announcement. "I'm here because my wife thinks I'm unhappy." "Are you unhappy?" Ed asked. Ben replied with an emphatic, "No, but everyone around me is. My job is to take care of my family. I do that day and night, so why should they complain?"

Ben had a 9mm Smith & Wesson gun "at the ready" in his bedroom drawer. Every night, Ben's willingness to aggressively defend his family fulfilled his role as protector. Then he would wake up every morning and head to work to assume his role as provider.

In that first counseling session, Ben kept up his emotional shields with Ed. "I'm fine," he claimed.

But Ben wasn't fine.

A few therapy sessions later, Ben admitted to Ed that he was exhausted and stressed "beyond belief." He worked all the time in order to provide for his family. His wife called herself a "work widow" and his kids gave up expecting to do things with their dad.

"My father was a lazy bum," Ben said. "At school, they laughed at me because of my patched-up clothes. Now, I'm giving my family so much more than I could ever imagine. But no matter what I do for them, it's not enough."

Ben's intention was to love and care for his family—to be a good husband and father. That wasn't the problem. The problem stemmed from a narrow expression of his masculinity. Ben represented the way confined masculinity shapes many men's lives—as well as the limitations of this version of manhood. In this chapter, we will define what we mean by confined masculinity in greater detail, describing the beliefs, behaviors, and consequences of this approach to being a man. We also will explore the roots of this unhealthy, outdated, and threatening version of masculinity.

Why "Confined" Masculinity?

People have been debating the nature of what it means to be a man for thousands of years. The ancient Greeks themselves had multiple, sometimes conflicting masculine ideals. There is the concept of the brave, strong hero who ventures forth on adventures and conquests—captured by the figure of Odysseus in the classic epics *The Iliad* and *The Odyssey*. But the Greeks displayed a range of masculine models in their pantheon of male deities, including Zeus, the all-powerful ruler; Ares, the god of war; Apollo, the god of reason and moral virtue; and Dionysus, the god of pleasure, awe, intuition, and ecstasy.

Definitions of masculinity—that is to say, male gender roles—have differed across cultures and changed over the course of human existence. For example, at the time of the American founding fathers, the culture encouraged intimate friendships between men—two male friends strolling arm in arm, sharing dreams and anxieties, would likely have raised no eyebrows.[1]

Reflecting that reality, Division 51 of the American Psychological Association (APA)—the wing devoted to the study of men and boys—no longer refers to masculinity as a singular, fixed concept. Division 51 of APA now uses the term "masculinities" to indicate that there are many ways men live within and express manhood.

If you survey the landscape of masculinities and words used to describe the ways men are conditioned to live their lives, you will find phrases ranging from "toxic masculinity" to "caveman masculinity" to "traditional masculinity" to "noble masculinity."

We landed on the phrases "confined masculinity" and "liberating masculinity" to describe where masculinity has been and where it is headed. We chose the terms for a number of reasons. First, they are grounded in the work of Japanese psychiatrist Shoma Morita (1874–1938). He developed what is called Morita therapy, an action-oriented approach to counseling that blends Western and Eastern principles. Morita made a distinction between the "confined self" and the "extended self." The confined self is self-absorbed and excessively preoccupied with one's own needs. It's a mind entangled in subjective fears. Morita believed the confined self was the road to neurosis or poor emotional health.[2]

Finiteness and Scarcity

The term "extended self" used by Morita describes positive mental health through connection, compassion, and service to others. We'll talk more about the extended self, and our related concept of liberating masculinity, in the next chapter.

Morita's concept of the confined self, with its "me" focus and fearful outlook, captures key features of the way men and women have been socialized to think about manhood for many centuries.

Another reason we selected the term "confined masculinity" is that this is a masculinity defined by its limitations. It is centered on restrictions regarding deep-seated beliefs about manliness—about what roles men "should or should not" play, how men perform those roles, in what domains men can act, and for whom. There is also an underlying sense of finiteness and scarcity associated with this concept of masculinity. The mindset of scarcity—about things ranging from resources to sex to status—is intertwined with a fixed worldview. For confined men, a fundamental mental inflexibility creates anxiety around change and ambiguity, as well as confusion around sexuality and the feminine.

Before we delve more deeply into what confined masculinity looks like, it's important to note that some women also subscribe to this version of manhood. To succeed in realms where men have had more power, some women have adopted the attitudes and actions of confined masculinity. Women also can expect men to fit the contours of a constrained concept of manliness. They can reinforce confined masculinity in the way they praise, reward, slight, shame, and punish men—sometimes sending mixed signals. Take Ben's case. Even though his wife wanted him to spend more meaningful time with her, she also wanted Ben to be a successful breadwinner. Such contradictory messages can raise tricky questions for men, especially how to balance winning the bread with having enough time and energy to break bread with loved ones.

We also want to acknowledge that confined masculinity represents a node on a continuum of masculinities. Virtually all men have been exposed to and influenced by this forceful ideology, but that doesn't mean they adopt it wholesale. Growing numbers of men and women are challenging confined masculinity—in large part because it doesn't work in the world that's emerging.

What Is Confined Masculinity?

Confined masculinity identifies three main roles for men: the protector, the provider, and the conqueror. These are the central archetypes or standard models available to men under traditional views of what a "real" man is. These archetypes have ancient origins and tend to be universal across cultures. They hold value because they speak to timeless human experiences and adaptations. But in each man's life these archetypes play out in ways that are influenced by time and place. And, like everything else in psychology and biology, there are always individual differences. By keeping individual differences in mind, we can apply the archetypes to our lives, knowing their place is in the realm of the imagination.

In fantasy, literature, and popular culture, the protector has been the knight, the soldier, the defender of the home—as Ben saw himself with his Smith & Wesson. Similarly, the provider has been the farmer, the merchant, the man who brings home the bacon and enables the good life for his family. The conqueror has been the king, the high school quarterback, the corporate-ladder climber, the lady "killer"—the alpha male who vanquishes foes, controls his surroundings, and gets the girl. Confined masculinity makes little room for other roles, like the sensitive lover, the sage, the spiritual seeker and the healer.

A tightly confined approach to manhood prescribes a limited number of ways men can perform their gender roles. Think of this in terms of the "how." A reliance on competition, aggressiveness, physical courage, and arrogant confidence are the central *how* characteristics. Confined men view and treat virtually everyone as competitors in a contest. They are expected to "man up" and be brave in all circumstances, and to exhibit no vulnerability—which would be a sign of weakness. Confined masculinity dodges other ways of relating and moving through the world, including curiosity, compassion, and cooperation.

Similarly, confined men operate within a narrow *where*. Under confined masculinity, men find themselves limited to external realms. These domains include the personal arenas of the physical and sexual as well as the public arenas of fortune and social status. The ideal man is strong and sexually potent. He is rich, and holds prominence in the eyes of others. A man's internal life is often sidelined because it may reveal vulnerability and thus threaten his status. Confined masculinity tends to wall off the landscape of spirit and emotions—including the range of feelings that accompany interpersonal and intimate relationships. As a result, a confined man can be unaware of the needs of his soul or psyche.

A confined masculinity also restricts a man's circle of care and concern to just himself, his family, and a a limited number of others. A confined man may identify with particular geographic communities, or those that share characteristics such as race, political ideology, religious beliefs, or even the fan base for a professional sports team. But his sense of communal humanity tends not to extend broadly. There is little attention to wider circles of people, or to his connection to the web of life on earth overall.

Confined masculinity is about finiteness. It creates a cage within which a man paces back and forth. He's kept limited, isolated and separate. Confined masculinity constricts the imagination because the concept of manhood is plugged into preset cultural ideas. It's like always coloring inside the lines. The epitome of confined masculinity is the fantasy of a "self-made man"—denying our need for and dependence on others. Confined masculinity creates unhealthy illusions when it calls for self-sufficiency and independence—often leading to loneliness.

Related to the emphasis on discreteness is how the classically confined man tends to view things as fixed, including talents, intelligence, gender roles, human nature, and what a "real man" is. There's little room for growth in these and other areas. Additionally, confined masculinity operates from a mindset of scarcity. A confined man sees the world as defined by sparse, limited resources that must be fought over in an endless series of zero-sum games. As a result, confined masculinity carries with it a fundamental anxiety based on a persistent state of fear: Will I get enough? Enough food for myself, my family, my people? Enough money? Enough status?

The Confined Masculinity Crouch...
and Other Consequences

The underlying fear, combined with the conqueror role, competitiveness, and limited circle of care for others, effectively puts confined men in a defensive crouch. Confined men are vigilant, poised to lash out—while their coiled-up stance prevents them from seeing their surroundings fully. This lack of vision means that confined men are without a full range of physical, emotional, and relational responses. Confined men, for example, often fail to notice the emotional signals from others that require sensitive and comforting responses. Because it truncates emotional intelligence, confinement limits vital affective skills.

The confined masculinity "crouch" shows up as distrust as well as overreaction to perceived threat and fear. In response to real or perceived threats, confined men are prone to dominate, avoid, shut down, or appease others. This leads to a paradox: confined men often take up a lot of emotional and physical space. Their very confined-ness leads them to spill outside of appropriate boundaries. They can bluster through business meetings or bully and shame others into submission to make sure they "win the day." And yet, confined men also end up with too little space and airtime. When men who have accepted the premise of constant competition consistently fail to rise to the top of the heap, they tend to accept the authority of those who do. They are predisposed to tolerate, appease, and befriend bullies—or to retreat into a profound passivity.

Call it the crouch-couch effect. If men find they can't cope with the ever-present threat of losing status and feeling inadequate, they can fall back into resignation and apathy. They may surrender to vegging out in front of a TV or computer screen. A man's emotional emptiness and lonely feelings can lead him to give in to destructive habits and empty pleasures, such as an addiction to pornography. In other words, confined masculinity can lead both to overbearing behavior and meek withdrawal. These are two sides of the same crouch.

Another consequence of confined masculinity is a tendency toward self-absorption. "I'm not much, but I'm all I think about," one of Ed Adams's patients joked. Though his statement revealed a measure of self-awareness and humility, it nonetheless acknowledged the way he—and many other men—obsess about themselves.

Even when men work hard, long hours in the service of their family, their focus can remain largely on themselves. Providing a good living and home can be as much about "keeping up with the Joneses"—or beating them—as it is about caring for family. Similarly, the achievements of children are often seen as a reflection of the success of their parents. This dynamic helps explain the manic way some men cheer and jeer at youth sports events. How well Susie performs on the field either burnishes or bruises the ego of her father.

Bottled Up

Anyone who has suffered through a soccer game next to an obnoxious, screaming dad knows that this projection is not healthy for anyone—including the confined man himself. In fact, even as confined masculinity makes men prone to self-centeredness, it also prevents men from connecting to themselves in a positive way. Natural feelings of hurt or disappointment or sadness are defined as signs of weakness. They give rise to shame. And that is only magnified by keeping all these emotions within.

"Because of the way many men have been brought up—to be self-sufficient and able to take care of themselves—any sense that things aren't okay needs to be kept secret," says Fredric Rabinowitz, PhD, a psychologist at the University of Redlands in California who helped steward the new APA guidelines on treating men and boys. "Part of what happens is men who keep things to themselves look outward and see that no one else is sharing any of the conflicts that they feel inside. That makes them feel isolated. They think they're alone. They think they're weak."[3]

All the pent-up feelings in confined masculinity can end up expressing themselves in a variety of ways. They show up in self-medication and substance abuse, in bursts of anger, in depression, anxiety, isolation—and sometimes in violence.

We noted above that a social aspect of confined masculinity is its inclination toward acquiescing to those in power. Another communal effect is that it conditions men to join together in opposition to people outside their limited circle. That is, confined men are susceptible to ganging up against people defined as "others" based on characteristics such as perceived racial, religious, geographic, and political differences.

This opposition to the other can be particularly problematic when it comes to misogyny and intolerance of people who don't fit inside strict sexual norms. "Misogyny" means contempt for women, and it reflects a combination of female objectification, sexual frustration, and a sense that men are fundamentally better than women. Intolerance of people with sexual variations refers to fear and hatred of same-sex relationships and other non-standard choices around sexuality and gender. These choices include bisexuality, transsexuality, and identifying as nonbinary—declining to identify as either male or female.

Stuck with Sexism and Intolerance

Given its limited conceptions of manhood, confined masculinity fosters sexism and intolerance of sexual variation. The conquering, stoic, self-sufficient, sexually potent provider— the warrior-patriarch—all but requires a woman to be his submissive subject. And a fixed conception of masculinity often leads confined men to define gay men as being deviant or "sick"—perhaps as a result of the fear of non-standard sexuality stirring within themselves.

So confined men are inclined to see themselves as superior to and at odds with women and people with unconventional sexuality. They may express this contempt through physical aggression individually. And as accounts of mass rape and group assaults on sexual minorities over the centuries have attested, confined men are capable of carrying out such violence in a collective way as well.

The beliefs, behaviors, and consequences we observe in confined masculinity dovetail with other analyses of men's traditional gender roles. Consider, for example, the conclusions of scholar Robert Brannon in his seminal study of American men. Writing in 1976, he identified four key elements of masculinity:

- No Sissy Stuff (anti-femininity)
- The Big Wheel (status and achievement)
- The Sturdy Oak/Male Machine (inexpressiveness and independence)
- Give 'Em Hell (adventurousness and aggressiveness)[4]

Brannon's observations about the dominant way of being a man have held largely true through the first two decades of the twenty-first century. We believe it is useful to locate these four aspects of manhood within the overarching concept of confinement. The confined masculinity model frames opposition to femininity, focus on power, stoicism, and combativeness as limited options. In effect, these "man-rules" act as invisible walls of a box, as unseen bars of a cage. As we will see, it's possible to be liberated from this constricted view of manhood.

The Roots of Confined Masculinity

Where does confined masculinity come from? How did we arrive at a cramped version of manhood that typically features hyper-aggression, extreme competitiveness, stoicism, and independence to the point of isolation? A masculinity in which a man's self-worth depends almost exclusively on besting others, where vulnerability is off-limits, and where women and those with non-standard sexualities are inferior?

Some argue that the reason men are aggressive is because "that's just the way men are" or because "men have always been this way."

Neither point is true.

Let's look first at the past. Based on the 6,000 years or so of recorded human history, it's easy to assume our species has always had largely fixed gender roles in which men are combative, insensitive, and individualistic—driven to "get the girl" and amass personal power and riches. This view of the macho, Machiavellian male captures several millennia of humankind succinctly, but it does not define what men were like before recorded history.[5]

For tens of thousands of years, our *Homo sapiens* ancestors lived in hunter-gatherer societies. And scholars generally agree that these early men and women seemed prone to share power and were likely to engage in caring, "prosocial" behavior.[6]

A number of observers view the rise of agriculture as pivotal in reshaping gender roles. One theory points to the emergence of the animal-drawn plow in particular as critical to the polarization of the sexes. Working a plow behind a draft animal wasn't suitable for pregnant women, because it gave rise to miscarriages. Scholar Ken Wilber argues that the animal-drawn plow led, in large part, to the domestication of women's roles—and to more economically productive, public, and ultimately powerful roles for men.[7]

The Way We Were: A Quiz

Do you think the following statements are true or false?

1. According to scientists, the earliest human societies are likely to have been egalitarian.
   True ☐   False ☐

2. Sexual equality is not a recent idea. Anthropologists suggest that it has been the norm for humans for most of our evolutionary history.
   True ☐   False ☐

3. Sexual equality may have been an evolutionary advantage for early human societies, as it would have fostered wider-ranging social networks and friendlier cooperation between unrelated individuals.
   True ☐   False ☐

The correct answer to all three statements is True. If you answered any of these correctly, then you too may wonder what happened to us "modern" peoples.

Based on Robert Sapolsky, "Peace Among Primates," *Greater Good Magazine*, September 1, 2007.

It's possible that when agrarian settlements became permanent and grew in population, the most aggressive men were able to seize social and political control—establishing autocratic, hierarchical male traditions that continue to this day.[8]

Just because the history of human civilization has largely

been a patriarchal one, that doesn't mean men have always been defined by a confined masculinity. If anything, the past several thousand years appear to have been an aberration. The full story of our species suggests men are capable of very different beliefs and behaviors. As scholar Paul Gilbert put it in the foreword to this book, "When social environments are benign then male psychology is also benign."

The Nature of Man

Still, some claim that the truest expression of male psychology is dominance—the alpha male who rules those weaker than himself. As this logic goes, men are naturally belligerent thanks to the power of testosterone, which is associated with aggressive behavior and sexual impulses. But it is too simplistic to claim that this hormone determines how men think and act. "Study after study has shown that when you examine testosterone levels when males are first placed together in the social group, testosterone levels predict nothing about who is going to be aggressive,"[9] writes Robert Sapolsky, a professor of biology and neuroscience at Stanford University.

A study that Sapolsky coauthored points to how socialization can outpower biology—and to the way gender roles can change quickly. While researching baboon behavior, Sapolsky observed a particular group of the primates feeding from a rubbish dump that contained poisoned meat. Because dominant males always ate first, they consumed the tainted meat and died off. Those of us who assign great importance to testosterone and the supposedly fixed "law of the jungle" might have predicted that new alpha males would rise to fill the vacant slots. That didn't happen. Instead, the group became far less aggressive, more egalitarian, and more affiliative. In other words, when the dominant males that created the atmosphere of aggressive competitiveness perished, the structure they created perished with them.[10]

Sapolsky's baboon study has parallels in research on differences between the sexes. Despite the popular notion that men and women are so unlike as to be from different planets, the science suggests we have more in common than not. Research demonstrates that the most statistically significant and predictable differences between men and women are small. A major study of variations between the sexes in 2005 discovered that men and women are basically alike in terms of personality, cognitive ability, and leadership. Psychologist Janet Shibley Hyde, PhD, of the University of Wisconsin-Madison, found only a few main differences: men could throw farther, were more physically aggressive, masturbated more, and held more positive attitudes about sex within uncommitted relationships.

It may be tempting to see the findings around aggression and sex as confirming gender stereotypes. But Hyde's study undermines that conclusion. She found that gender differences seem to depend on the context in which they were measured. For example, after participants in one experiment were situated such that they could not be identified as male or female, none conformed to stereotypes about their sex when given the chance to be aggressive. On the contrary, they did the opposite of what would be expected—women were more aggressive and men were more passive.[11]

It's too easy to hide behind the false notion that men and women are forever condemned to be alienated from one another. It's useful to acquire an allergic reaction when people say, "he's just being a man" or, "that's the way women are."

In other words, DNA isn't destiny. Men's mindsets and learned gender roles play a major role in how we behave. The mindsets and roles of confined masculinity haven't always been the standard for human beings, but they have shaped a male-dominated history over the past six thousand years or so. This history has been marked by aggression, competition, separateness, and emotional inhibition.

Taking the Measure of Confined Masculinity

It would be a mistake to condemn confined masculinity altogether. Elements of the ideology, such as the conqueror figure, stoicism, and focus on the material realm, have combined to lead men to great feats of exploration, ingenuity, and athleticism. Confined men have probed the corners of the earth, erected cathedrals, and pushed the limits of human physical ability, often enduring great hardship in the process. The provider and protector roles have contributed to good-hearted personas such as the knight and the gentleman, and to related values such as honor, valor, and virtue. Influenced by confined masculinity, men have sacrificed life and limb to bravely combat tyranny and oppression.

Another positive of confined masculinity is that it is a counterweight to ideologies that diminish the individual. Self-reliance and personal ambition also have generated great advances in artistic expression and contributed to technological and material progress.

That said, confined masculinity has never been an ideal approach for being a man. Throughout the ages, wise souls from the Buddha to Jesus to Mohandas Gandhi to Martin Luther King Jr.—not to mention many women visionaries—have challenged its tenets of aggression, materialism, and selfishness. Artists and poets have questioned the limitations of confined masculinity and expressed the suffering of men whose lives have been defined by this constrained male ethos. And many men and woman have bravely refused to accept the heterosexual norms prescribed by a traditional, narrow manhood.

Today more than ever, confined masculinity is under fire. Put simply, confined manhood doesn't work for the twenty-first century. Confined masculinity now limits and damages men as individuals, in our family and friend circles, in our organizations, and in our global society.

Most men know there's something wrong and deeply restrictive about following the traditional man-rules to a *t*. They gravitate toward liberating masculinity—if for no other reason than the fact that confined masculinity doesn't work in their lives. These men are bigger than what society has largely told them to be.

Ed Adams was asked what his years of working with men in therapy and groups has taught him. His short answer is that "the love and sacrifice I see men capable of giving to others is literally awe inspiring."

Both authors believe in the goodness and humanity of

men. That is why we encourage a vision of masculinity that frees men and unleashes their full potential. And why we are eager to help men move away from a limited version of manhood that has run its course.

Ben's story from earlier in this chapter illustrates how a good and well-intentioned man experienced the restrictions of confined masculinity. By taking his provider role so seriously, Ben brought himself out of poverty, and later prevented his family from backsliding into deprivation. His children never had to wear patched-up clothes as he had. They avoided the humiliation he suffered on the school yard.

And yet the rules of confined masculinity did not fully serve Ben or his family. In fact, those rules created more enduring problems than they prevented. And that is becoming more and more true for men stuck in confined masculinity—as well as for the people around them.

But there's hope.

We now know that many of our confined ideas about masculinity may be commonly shared but they are not fixed. We can change. And we can create a more egalitarian, cooperative, and safer world.

Now let's explore a masculinity that helps us build that world.

THINGS TO PONDER AND DO

CURIOSITY: What rules of confined masculinity have you assumed are valid? Can you pinpoint an event or encounter when this version of manhood influenced you?

COURAGE: Can you acknowledge the ways confined masculinity harms you and others?

COMPASSION: Can you forgive yourself for actions you took while under the influence of a confined masculinity? Can you better understand a man in your life who hurt you while operating from confined masculinity?

CONNECTION: Is there someone in your life who has reached out to you, but whom you shunned out of anger or fear, or because of some other reason? Can you reach out to them now?

COMMITMENT: Can you pledge to move away from the attitudes and actions of confined masculinity? Can you commit to challenging men who hurt others?

The Release

2 The Way Forward: Liberating Masculinity

For an understanding of liberating masculinity, meet Jeff.

Jeff was in deep distress about his troubled marriage. He began his psychotherapy sessions with coauthor Ed Adams feeling as if his emotions were "beaten with a rubber hose." Jeff was searching for guidance to help him change and become more open to life and love.

Even when his marriage ended, Jeff continued to believe that his only source of comfort could come from any recognition, kindness, or appreciation from his ex-wife. It was hard for him to accept the fact that his ex-wife was the last person who would be willing to comfort him. This obsessive need set off a looping cycle of emotional hurt that he could not seem to stop.

Jeff's misery was magnified when his ex-wife remarried and moved far away with their two children, ages five and twelve.

Six months later, Jeff announced in a session, "I have some important news." He told Ed that his ex-wife's new husband had been diagnosed with stage 4 cancer. As he was sharing the story, Jeff showed an unconscious but discernable smirk.

"What was that grin about?" Ed asked. Jeff was honest enough to admit that he felt a sense of satisfaction knowing that he was not the only one "in a world of hurt."

Then came Ed's challenge. "You tell me you want to become more open, loving, and compassionate, yet you delight in someone being given a dreadful death sentence." After further discussion, Ed urged Jeff to write a compassionate letter to his ex-wife and her husband and to bring the letter to their next session. "This letter-writing exercise will help us explore the more loving man and father you say you wish to become," Ed explained.

At the start of their next session, Ed asked Jeff if he'd brought the draft of the letter. "No," he beamed, "but I did bring a copy of the letter I already sent." Here is what it said:

Dear Mary and John:

I heard about the heartbreaking diagnosis that must be very painful for each of you. I am truly sorry this is happening in your life together. We all deserve to live a full and long life. Although I can't change the medical realities you face, I know I can help.

You will need time together and you will need to know the kids are safe as you attend to all the necessary medical procedures. I will help with the kids. I can come to you or the kids can come to me. I will help as best I can financially and I will be there with or without any prior notice. In addition, I will help the kids cope and understand the difficulties we all face.

Again, I am sorry for your health issue and I hope that everything eventually turns out great for both of you. I will keep you in my positive thoughts.

Sincerely,

Jeff

Jeff made good on his promise. He was a consistent source of support and comfort throughout the illness and untimely

Pop Culture and Liberating Masculinity

The stories we find in popular culture often are variations on the archetypal hero's journey. As scholar Joseph Campbell noted in his classic work *The Hero with a Thousand Faces*, protagonists typically follow a path of adventure, struggle, transformation, and reunion. Within this mythic pattern, though, the stories we tell ourselves can take on the flavor of the times. The overall structure of the hero's journey may be stable, but exactly how he or she moves through challenges will change in response to an era's values and social conditions.

There are signs that pop culture today is reflecting and reinforcing the shift from an outdated version of manhood to a better, newer model. In particular, changes in the nature of widely viewed movies and TV shows in the early twenty-first century suggest a society transitioning from a confined masculinity to a liberating one.

Look below for stories about superheroes and knights to see how masculinity is being reinvented in popular culture.

death of his ex-wife's husband. His support also allowed him to spend more time with his children. As he looks back, Jeff values the man he became throughout that stressful time. He believes it served as the essential glue that continues to hold an enduring bond with his children. This positive outcome was possible because Jeff turned his self-absorbed feelings into kind action directed toward others.

Jeff's story captures one man's journey from a confined masculinity toward a liberating masculinity. He moved beyond egocentric, petty, bitterness to big-hearted compassion. And his choice to connect in cooperation rather than stew in isolation helped him achieve his desire to be a vital and involved father.

Jeff is not alone in embracing a liberating masculinity and in finding freedom and success by responding to the needs of others. In this chapter, we describe what we mean by liberating masculinity by spelling out the beliefs, behaviors, and consequences of this way of being a man.

Why "Liberating Masculinity"?

As mentioned earlier in our discussion of confined masculinity, we chose the terms "confined" and "liberating" in part because of their grounding in the work of psychiatrist Shoma Morita. Morita's notion of the "extended self" includes an awareness of the needs of others and behavior that "leads to service." We opted to modify Morita's terminology by using "liberating" rather than "extended." We believe "liberating masculinity" better conveys the way this version of manhood involves an emancipation from the restrictions imposed by confined masculinity. An inflexible obedience to traditional "man-rules" effectively imprisons men. Liberating masculinity speaks to the way this alternative approach breaks men out of what's sometimes called the "man box."

We also believe the word "liberating," more than "extended," speaks to how a masculinity centered on a "me and we" perspective is about two kinds of freedom. Liberating masculinity releases a man from living a cramped life. At the same time, this masculine ethos calls on him to help others live freer, fuller, and more meaningful lives.

That second sense of liberation, especially, dovetails with Morita's view of the extended self. And we will often talk about liberating masculinity as involving men extending and expanding their self-awareness such that they become more mindful of the welfare and needs of others. Liberating masculinity is fundamentally about expanding and developing in multiple directions. These include reaching outward to connect, understand, and help others as well as elevating one's consciousness to comprehend a more complex, interdependent world. It also implies "growing downward" by developing deep roots in a solid foundation of personal morals and self-awareness.

The downward growth is an *inward* expansion. That is, liberating masculinity not only frees men to express themselves outwardly in new ways, it enables them to enjoy a richer interior life as well. This is very different from the self-absorption of confined masculinity, which is primarily focused on fulfilling basic desires like sexual satisfaction, social status, and a sizable salary. For the liberating man, internal growth has to do with greater self-knowledge, including heightened recognition of one's desires, one's unique path, and one's fundamental link to all of life. This "down and in" growth results in a greater sense of rootedness, belonging, and purpose. It gives life to becoming a multifaceted man.

We also chose the "-ing" ending to "liberating" to convey the kinetic, dynamic nature of this manhood. "Liberating masculinity" has definition and clear characteristics. Yet it also enables a man to continually emerge and develop by sensing and responding to the evolving conditions in which he finds himself. While confined masculinity tends to be fixed and cramped, liberating masculinity is open, more fluid, and freer to adapt, change, mature, and ripen.

Defining Liberating Masculinity

Liberating masculinity is a spacious version of masculinity, one that makes room for ongoing growth. It directs a man toward the opposite end of the continuum from confined masculinity. Liberating masculinity frees a man to play a larger variety of roles. Besides widening the *what* a man can be, liberating masculinity also broadens the *how, where,* and *for whom.*

With respect to the roles a man can assume, liberating masculinity embraces the multiple dimensions that humans possess and the many archetypes available to men. These include the options central to confined masculinity—provider, protector, and conqueror. But it also enables men to embody additional roles, including but not limited to lover, sage, artist, adventurer, healer, and little boy.

To get a sense of how these can coexist and cooperate, try this thought experiment:

Imagine a large round table. The provider, protector, and conqueror dimensions of yourself are sitting with you as a personal council of advisors. Now, let's imagine you want to go on a weekend getaway with your friend or partner. You process this idea through the eyes of your provider and protector. Within seconds the idea is dismissed. You will hear yourself thinking about loss. Your judging and negative internal voices will gladly provide objections centered on time and money, and how some work projects are coming due that need your full attention. Goodbye, pleasure trip.

Now, reimagine this scenario with an increased number of advisors. At the table would be your king, visionary, benevolent warrior, artist, healer, lover, poet, magician, politician, adventurer, shaman, sage, and comic selves. Also present is your little boy. And let's not forget the shadow parts we all hide from others, like your saboteur and your angry warrior. Honoring a variety of archetypes, or facets of self, makes for a very different decision-making process, and may lead to surprising outcomes.

The adventurer plans the trip while the benevolent warrior figures out how to afford it. The healer reminds you that time away from work is needed and the lover agrees that you and your partner "need to get away from it all" and reconnect romantically. And so on.

When we are making an important life decision, but only process through the lens of limited dimensions of our self, then we'll have a limited outcome. When we fail to pay

Expanding Superheroes

The twentieth century had plenty of superhero movies and TV shows, and they tended to have confined masculine motifs. They focused on solo figures like Batman and Superman. And the Caped Crusader and Man of Steel were men of few words when it came to emotional honesty—sometimes comically so. But in recent decades, the genre has moved in a cooperative, expressive direction.

The ultra-popular movie series *The Avengers* epitomized the shift. Individual heroes like Captain America, Black Widow, and Iron Man team up and take advantage of complementary powers. Male Avengers also have stood out both for sharing authority with female heroines and for their sensitivity. They display romantic affection and parental tenderness—and, in the case of Captain America, even lead a grief counseling session.

Today's superheroes may be as physically strong and powerful as ever. But their masculinity has expanded. Galactic guardians now are willing to work collaboratively and let their emotional guard down—showing they're not just heroic but also fully human.

attention to our fuller dimensions, we risk becoming stale. We may think we're happy, but those around us will see how stuck we really are. When we recognize, appreciate, and engage our complexity, we also expand and liberate our masculine identity.

In his work as a therapist, coauthor Ed Adams often finds that depressed men constrain their own dimensionality—often because they don't recognize that it exists. That depression may be revealing a strong desire to live unlived lives. And a yearning for greater satisfaction. For example, the lover inside a betrayed man longs for a relationship with deep trust. Or a man in an unfulfilling job wants a career that taps his adventurer spirit.

Men often walk through life hoping to find fulfillment while disregarding their unlived lives. This is what Ben—described in the last chapter—began to realize about himself. He was a depressed man unable to hear his inner voice pleading to actually "be alive."

In effect, Ben had been asleep to his own complexity, dismissing his deeper desires. He had dulled his awareness of the full range and dimensions of his interior life. His imagination of himself was truncated or non-existent—and you can't make something real unless it first exists in the imagination. Still, when dimensions are ignored, they eventually rebel, demanding to be expressed.

In Ben's case, his body, mind, and soul wanted him to pay attention to his complexity in order to live a larger, deeper, and more meaningful life—not to mention a life with greater positive impact. The consequence of not doing so can create symptoms or havoc like deep unhappiness, depression, or a failed marriage—and not just because of a man's internal turmoil. Those around a confined man suffer as well. Ben's wife, for example, was longing to be wooed by Ben's "lover" archetype.

More Ways and Means

So, liberating masculinity permits a man to embody more dimensions and archetypes. It also enables him to perform those roles in more creative ways, in more arenas, and for a wider circle of people and living beings.

When it comes to the *how*, to the strategies and behaviors available to men, a liberating man is comfortable but not satisfied with the ways of confined masculinity—its focus on competition, physical courage, confidence, and achievement. Liberating masculinity adds a variety of behaviors to the mix. These include curiosity, courage to challenge one's beliefs, compassion, connection, and a commitment to personal growth. Liberating masculinity enables a man to confront rivals bravely, but he also knows that an adversarial stance is not his only option. He is better equipped to learn about others, to empathize with them, and to cooperate.

Similarly, liberating masculinity incorporates and transcends the domains where confined masculinity operates. A liberating man aims to be physically and intellectually strong, sexually satisfied, financially secure, and socially esteemed. He also is free to venture with courage into the territories of emotions and the psyche. He is able to follow the yearnings of his soul. His ability to experience and communicate about feelings, intuition, and spiritual matters does not hinder him in the landscapes of sex, physicality, fortune, and social status. On the contrary, liberating masculinity frees and invites him to experience greater highs and deeper depths in his sex life, his body, his work, and his relationship to the wider society.

Finally, liberating masculinity widens his circle of caring

for others. He begins with the people for whom a confined man reserves his affections and loyalties: himself, his nuclear family, and a limited group of others who may share family, racial, religious, national, or other characteristics. A liberating masculinity extends a man's concerns ever outward, to encompass people of all backgrounds and beliefs. Indeed, a liberating man appreciates the value of extending to others the freedoms and richness of life he gets to experience. He shares Martin Luther King Jr.'s view that "no one is free until we all are free." Similarly, a liberating man comes to treasure all life on earth and understands that all life deserves respect. To him, all human beings make up a single family, and we must act as responsible stewards of the living planet that is our home.

Connected for Good

Liberating masculinity is virtuous and relational. It is virtuous because it espouses positive actions that are of benefit to both the self and others; and it's relational because it recognizes that everything is interconnected.

Liberating masculinity operates from core beliefs that are both ancient and new. For example, it still sees men as warriors—but now the enemy isn't other people, the enemy is hatred and division. Men still possess power—but use that energy to create harmony and equality. Plus, the potency of men is channeled to give birth to strategies that relieve suffering and protect our environment. Men provide not only through financial support but also by being emotionally available to their loved ones. And men solve difficult personal

Dethroning Confined Masculinity

A striking feature of twenty-first-century pop culture is increased complexity. Complicated storylines and characters who do not fit neatly into "good guy" or "bad guy" categories have been central to megahit TV series like *The Sopranos, Breaking Bad,* and *The Wire.* These "prestige TV" programs, in effect, have chipped away at the simplistic, us-versus-them, black-and-white thinking of confined masculinity. They also have introduced topics once considered taboo to men holding conventional beliefs about manhood, such as the mental health problems experienced by Tony Soprano.

Game of Thrones, arguably the most popular TV show of the early twenty-first century, offered morally nuanced characters as well as new models of male identity. The medieval fantasy show's conclusion in particular suggested the rise of liberating masculinity in our cultural consciousness. Jon Snow, the main male protagonist, makes a heart-wrenching sacrifice to prevent a tyrannical ruler from taking the iron throne. And rather than seize power himself, he chooses a life of service. Ultimately, a wise, ego-less, physically disabled young man is selected to lead. He's aided by a council consisting of a female warrior and male characters who defy heroic stereotypes.

The movement from confined masculinity to liberating masculinity is a hero's journey in itself. So it shouldn't be surprising that some men who cling to comfortable but outdated conceptions of what a "real man" is experience trauma, even regressions. Popular culture, though, is prodding the transformation along. It is mirroring the emergence of a new version of manhood. And it is helping to mold new generations of men with stories that say there is more to being a man than what we used to see on screen.

and global problems without blame, rage, fear, shaming, and violence. Liberating masculinity is a manhood that acknowledges distress, pain and suffering in ourselves and others. It accepts responsibility for the dark side of our masculinity and strives to lessen its impact. And liberating masculinity is soul-based: it reconnects manhood with the sacredness of life and service to others.

Liberating masculinity is a relation-centered manhood that embraces a "me and we" perspective. It goes beyond the self-absorbed "me" focus found in confined masculinity. In liberating masculinity, we place compassion and connection at the heart of essential masculine traits. Because of this, boys and men identify as guardians and stewards who protect and nurture our core values. As this vision of manhood is woven into our cultural mythos, society will begin to expect the expanding man to use his strength and courage in virtuous and relational ways.

Nathan's Liberation from Depression

Consider the story of Nathan, one of Ed Adams's patients. Nathan and his wife decided to separate and pursue divorce. Nathan was suddenly alone and felt a unique emotion in his life—depression. Eventually, he entered psychotherapy to find "some way to get out of my dark hole."

At the end of their sixth session, Ed gave Nathan homework. "I want you to take a dozen roses to the hospital during visiting hours," Ed told Nathan. "Give a rose to any patient who has no visitors and wish them well." This assignment evoked anxiety in Nathan, so he put off doing it for several weeks. But when he finally completed it, he called Ed to thank him. "For what?" Ed asked.

Nathan replied, "Each rose I gave away, and every smile it created, lifted my spirits. I decided I better stop feeling sorry for myself. I actually made others happy. This assignment squeezed out my depression."

In a compassionate, virtuous, and connecting way, Nathan's hour in the hospital shifted his personal psychology. His actions moved him from a "me" to a "me and we" perspective. Later, Nathan referred to that experience as the time the "roses kick-started a cure for my depression."

Just as Nathan did, a liberating man confronts his fears instead of hiding from them. He is willing to feel strong emotion and engage in difficult tasks and conversations. He is willing to love and be loved. He is open to awe and wonder—while still knowing that pain and suffering is inherent in all life. He understands that compassion and connection are manly.

Brian Ogawa, a Morita therapist and educator, maintains that the "extended self"—what we call "liberating masculinity"—does not deny our own life forces but is actually a way to find them.[1] The awareness that the self can be found in our relationships and attention and service to others has been a central thesis of religious and secular teachings for centuries. For example, in the Torah we read, "Let your compassion come to me that I may live." The New Testament tells us, "Do not look to your own interests, but each of you to the interests of the others." In the Quran, "compassion" is the most frequently occurring word. Theologian Desmond Tutu of South Africa touts the concept of *Ubuntu*, which translates roughly to "I am because we are."[2] And the Buddhist monk and teacher Geshe Kelsang Gyatso states:

> All the happiness that arises in this world
> Arises from wishing others to be happy.[3]

When a man is oriented toward "me and we," he sees that the needs and experiences of all others are valid and are no more or less important than his own. And so, he can enter any space understanding that he is not the most important person there. He knows that his actions and nonactions have consequences beyond himself. He poses no threat to the dignity of womanhood. He is emotionally generous and unafraid of intimacy and diversity.

Perhaps the bottom line is that liberating masculinity is unafraid to love.

What About "Me"?

But let's be clear: caring more about others doesn't mean one cares less about oneself. Every man matters, and taking charge of one's life is necessary. A liberating man maintains a sense of agency and is curious about his own inner life. It's a natural and beneficial right to understand and pursue our own needs, dreams, and desires. It is normal to protect and provide for those we care about most. Indeed, it's within those close family and friend connections that the "me" oriented man learns and grows into his "me and we" orientation. There's nothing wrong with a man actively pursuing to better himself, or seeking worldly pleasures like a new car, a bucket-list vacation, or a safe and comfortable home.

"Me" thinking becomes a problem when we dismiss the interconnection of life, or when the needs of others are marginalized. If we act as though our needs, safety, and aspirations are more important than those of others, we are, in Buddhist terms, "self-cherishing" as opposed to cherishing others.[4]

The male fantasy of the "rugged individual" makes it easy to forget that we depend upon each other. The meals we ate yesterday are the result of plants and animals giving up life in order to sustain our own. Every meal involves farmers, processors, truck drivers, grocery workers, cooks, and countless others willing to work to sustain us while providing resources for themselves and others. The fact that you can read is attributed to those who taught you how to read. When egocentric decisions dominate, good things are less likely to happen.

If proof of that statement is needed, we suggest you watch or listen to the news of the day and ask yourself, did that man or woman act virtuously? Did that story reflect compassion or self-absorption? If you do this exercise, you'll likely find that the differences between contained and liberating become quickly evident. No liberating man will walk into a Walmart and shoot everyone in sight. No liberating man will take pride in fomenting hatred, division, and vitriol toward others. No man living according to liberating masculinity will use his status and power to subjugate or sexually abuse others; nor does he fear those of other races or sexual identities.

Let's look again at Ben in the previous chapter. Ben was stuck in a "me" cycle of thought. His myopic view of himself as provider and protector was the focus of his attention.

The Time and Space Between

Two strangers found themselves seated next to each other on a flight to somewhere. One passenger sat by the window in seat B, while the other was in aisle seat A. Between each seat, a moveable armrest designed for comfort established a clear boundary between the two. If the armrest could talk, it would say, "Do not enter." Without question, this message was understood since neither passenger attempted any intrusion upon the other.

As the plane was nearing its final landing approach, a potent and persistent turbulence tossed the mighty jet to and fro. Everyone on the flight was terrified. Everyone faced their mortality. In a moment of deep humanity, the passenger in seat A reached over and firmly clutched the hand of the stranger in seat B. Suddenly, the armrest became intrusive, the boundaries inane. The need for human touch superseded conventional rules. In a time when contact was paramount, to suffer alone seemed foolish.

It made me question. Am I surrounded by armrests? Do I depend upon turbulence to justify intimacy? Is emotional disconnection killing my soul?

—E. M. ADAMS

Eventually, though, Ben came to see that his identity as provider and protector created a paradoxical effect. He wanted to feel appreciated for his providing and protecting behaviors, but instead he was emotionally disconnected, which generated feelings of alienation and resentment. But once Ben began to expand his inner dimensions and became more "we" oriented, his family happily responded because he was finally giving them what they needed—his love and attention. Ben's wife summed it up when she told him, "I feel married to you again."

Toxic Masculinity and the Liberating Man

"We" thinking takes a serious departure away from toxic masculinity. "Toxic masculinity" is the concept that "real men" must suppress emotions or deny feeling hurt or pain. A toxic man is determined to show how "hard" and invulnerable he is. And toxic masculinity justifies violence and shaming to demonstrate power and dominance.

We believe most men disdain the notion of being toxic. The very term shames men. Men are looking for permission to express a "me and we" model of masculinity without shame. Many men find deep satisfaction in helping others and feeling strong emotions. Men want to reclaim compassion and connection back into the male ethos. The poet Rainer Maria Rilke challenges us "to become world."[5] By this he means that we are all rowing in the same boat, so every action or nonaction any of us takes affects everyone else. The liberating man imagines and helps create a world that works in harmony for everyone on board. In short, men are not toxic but living within confined masculinity generates toxicity. Liberating masculinity is an elixir, one that heals men and everyone around them.

Men Mentoring Men

One of the places we've seen liberating masculinity in action is in the Men Mentoring Men group founded by coauthor Ed Adams. Here, he shares the story:

> Thirty years ago, I started a therapy group for men with the intention to connect and explore life issues through our masculine lens. Four brave men attended that initial session. I suggested that we will operate with only one rule: no man shames another. I applied this rule because I had witnessed the erosive power of shame in so many men. It shut men down. I explained that in order for us to explore and share our emotions and our common experiences, we must feel emotionally safe. That is, we must feel safe enough to allow ourselves to be vulnerable with each other. Shame prevents or kills psychological safety. We needed to listen, reflect, ask, wonder, question, and feel. We participated in creating a culture that encouraged a move from a dominant "me" perspective toward an expanded "me and we" point of view. I told the men that we were part of an experiment to see if this can be achieved.

> Over the past three decades, that small group of four men has evolved into a not-for-profit organization called Men Mentoring Men or M3. Today M3 has five ongoing groups and over a hundred active men of all different ages, beliefs, races, and sexual orientations. M3 has directly and indirectly touched the lives of countless men, women, and children they love. After thirty years, M3 is no longer an experiment because the results are in. It works.

Given the opportunity to dive deeply into life experiences, men find safety, comfort, and solace in the company of other men. A new member typically begins the M3 experience with doubt and trepidation. It takes courage to attend M3. I am often astonished by the men's ability to rise up to meet or exceed the group expectation to be emotionally open and vulnerable while also protecting emotional safety. I watch men demonstrate their courage, act on their compassion, and make decisions with the explicit intention of positively impacting others. As this shift occurs, many men report feeling happier, healthier, and more connected. But it's not only the men who profit. Their spouses, partners, children, friends, and colleagues also benefit from the deeper and more connected lives liberating masculinity provides.

The enormous power of the many support groups for men, like Men Mentoring Men, resides in helping participants move from a "me" to a "me and we" perspective. As mentioned before, the liberating man becomes more purpose-driven as he develops compassion and connection toward others. And as most military veterans know, the main mission in combat is to make sure your friends survive. Ed Adams's dad was a WWII veteran who fought on Guadalcanal. He told Ed that everyone was scared and miserable but, in order to survive, every man had to care for the other. It was an "all for one and one for all" mindset. "In that jungle, we only had each other to depend upon," he said.

M3 is one of many groups throughout the world that support men and those they love in "living healthier and happier lives." A competent men's group is a powerful and helpful way

The Best Medicine

Jerry was diagnosed with testicular cancer a few years after joining M3. He required surgery within days. He was rightfully terrified—but he was not alone. Many men in that situation would tell no one, choosing instead to suffer in isolation. But Jerry didn't hide his diagnosis, and word of his situation quickly spread within the M3 community. Then, the night before Jerry was to enter the hospital, Ed Adams called an emergency meeting for men to console and support him. With short notice, seventeen very busy men met with Jerry to connect and listen to his tearful fears.

After the successful surgery and throughout his rounds of chemotherapy, Jerry was contacted, encouraged, and loved by the men of M3. His body is cancer free today, and Jerry is grateful for the miracle of medicine. But Jerry maintains that it was the hope and comfort he received from the men that gave him the strength and will to prevail. "I look back and wonder if I would have the same outcome if the M3 support was missing," Jerry told his group with heartfelt appreciation. "I feel bad for men who go through difficult times alone. I know this because I often had chemotherapy treatments sitting next to very sad and isolated men."

Jerry's brush with cancer came with one significant benefit. As a result of his experience, Jerry committed himself to giving hope to others. He has provided empathy and support to other men facing difficult challenges in their life. Today, Jerry believes that compassion and connection are the best medicine—both to give and to get.

to affect men. If you can find a good men's group, give it a try. If no group exists in your area, consider starting one. (You'll find some resources later in this book.)

Moving from a confined male ethos toward liberating masculinity is not easy. The change process creates fear and confusion. There is a dearth of firm direction and leadership to guide men and give them permission to reinvent their masculinity, to modernize their way of being a man.

Still, the reinvention is underway. Throughout the United States and across the globe, men—with the support of women—are updating their beliefs and behaviors to adapt to our times.

In the next chapter we show how you can join them.

THINGS TO PONDER AND DO

CURIOSITY: From a low of 1 to a high of 10, where do you think you are on the continuum between confined and liberating masculinity?

COURAGE: Think of a man in your life who had the courage to express vulnerability. How did you feel experiencing his courage? Did you see him as less or more of a man because he opened up?

COMPASSION: Think of a time when you were in need of compassion and a man provided it for you. What happened? How did it feel? Was it a source of comfort?

CONNECTION: What blocks you from connecting with others with deep and important feelings? Are there any beliefs or fears that get in your way?

COMMITMENT: Decide on and promote "me and we" practices in your home and workplace. Can you create a habit of thinking about the needs of others as well as your own? How will you remind yourself to focus on others?

Five Flowers

3 How to Reinvent Your Masculinity: The Five Cs

How do you move toward a liberating masculinity? How does a man reinvent his own masculinity so he can experience and benefit from the liberating power of compassion and connection?

Books and other teachings can help. These can range from religious texts to self-help guides to inspiring memoirs, novels, and movies.

You also can think of men in your life whom you admire. What qualities make them good friends, good spouses, good fathers, good colleagues, good citizens? How do they show up, especially in difficult circumstances?

Or, think about legendary good men and the traits that make them iconic role models. These could be men like Jesus, Muhammad, Moses, and the Buddha, who inspired entire religious traditions. Or more recent virtuous men, such as Mohandas Gandhi, Martin Luther King Jr., and Nelson Mandela. Why are we drawn to their examples?

None of these "model men" lived perfect lives. Still, they all shared a commitment to kindness, benevolence, and a view of humanity as one interconnected family. They helped pave a path toward the liberating masculinity that is emerging and imperative in our times.

How do you walk that path today?

The path to liberating masculinity involves five key practices, which we call the "Five Cs." They are Curiosity, Courage, Compassion, Connection, and Commitment.

We believe all men can practice the Five Cs in order to move toward a liberating masculinity. And yet it's a lifelong quest, a process that never ends. There is always room to grow deeper, go further, learn more, and love more.

When men integrate each of these Five Cs into their lives, when they make a habit of these practices, the constraints of confined masculinity melt away. These men open up the cage of outdated man-rules and begin to live fuller, more effective, more satisfying lives.

In this chapter, we will discuss each of the Five Cs and offer concrete exercises that support each practice.

Curiosity

Men often provide answers but neglect to ask key questions.

Curiosity is the first C. It's about being in wonder and asking important, challenging, and probing questions, including ones that may make us uncomfortable. Here are some examples:

▸ What kind of man do I want to be?

▸ What responsibilities do I have to other people? To life itself?

▶ How have the man-rules I grew up with shaped and possibly limited my life?

Another example: can I ask for directions while driving?

You might be saying to yourself, even playfully: "Real men don't ask for directions!" The stereotype of the stubbornly lost man gets at why genuine curiosity is tough for men who live within confined masculinity. That version of manhood warns us not to seek help or reveal that we don't have all the answers in order to avoid feeling shame or inadequacy. We're taught to try to be "the smartest guy in the room" and to be self-sufficient.

To move past the constraints of confined masculinity, we need to honor and practice curiosity. Men need to ask existential as well as practical questions, looking in places they don't normally explore. We need to challenge stereotypes and not accept traditional male roles as "the way it is." By doing so we can learn, and we can develop a deeper awareness of ourselves and of others, as well as how we affect them.

Take this example from another patient of Ed Adams. We'll call him Michael. He came to see Ed when his marriage was in crisis: his wife had begun an affair. The infidelity was particularly painful to Michael because this was the second time he'd experienced such a violation. An earlier long-term partner had also cheated on him.

It would have been easy for Michael to blame both women for his troubles. After all, our culture of confined masculinity can frame women as untrustworthy, even emotionally dangerous. The confined framework also defines men whose wives have betrayed them as cuckolds—as lacking in manliness, as laughingstocks. But Michael didn't take the easy route of playing the victim, nor did he resort to self-lacerating shame. Instead, he got curious about his role in this pattern. "What's going on with me, that women are willing to cheat on me?" he asked Ed. "What am I doing or not doing that made my wife interested in straying outside the marriage?"

These are the kinds of difficult questions that allow for true growth at the individual, personal level. But such growth can happen in the work arena as well. A good example of curiosity in the organizational setting involves Jim Weddle, the former top executive of financial services firm Edward Jones.

When he was managing partner of Edward Jones some years ago, Weddle visited a group of branch office administrators. These are the folks who coordinate the operations of the firm's neighborhood offices and provide front-line service to customers.

One of these employees told Weddle that the financial advisor in her office often traveled to regional training events and returned with new ideas the administrator was supposed to adopt.

The administrator paused. Then she told Weddle, "If it's not something I want to do, and it's not my idea, it's not going to work."

Many CEOs would have treated her comment as insubordination. They might even have fired her. Not Weddle. Instead, he and his team used this as an opportunity to get curious about their training philosophy. And they decided to expand the offsite events to include branch office administrators like the woman who had spoken out.[1]

In one sense, this was a small shift. But it represented a big change from the confined masculinity mindset. That version of manhood tends to treat critical feedback as something to be deflected or parried—because admitting flaws or a lack of knowledge conveys weakness. Weddle effectively made himself vulnerable by acknowledging that the training system could be improved and considering how to make it better.

Curiosity is something that all men have access to as part of our common humanity. We are naturally inquisitive creatures. As children, as boys, we wonder why the sky is blue. What makes trees grow? How do airplanes fly? Why do our fathers act the way they do?

Unfortunately, by the time we are young adults much of this marveling has been shamed out of our system. We become afraid of asking a "stupid question." Confined masculinity makes matters worse by emphasizing knowing over learning, answers over questions, and authority over investigation.

Ed Adams's wife, Marilee Adams, has important insights here. She is the author of the book *Change Your Questions, Change Your Life*. Marilee notes that at every moment people have a fundamental choice: to adopt a "Judger" mindset or a "Learner" mindset. When we operate from the "Judger" perspective, we ask questions like: "Who's fault is it?" "What's wrong with me?" "What's wrong with them?" This reactive, blaming, win–lose approach comes straight out of the confined masculinity handbook, and it leads to apathy, self-loathing, and negativity toward others.

But if we choose to be "Learners," our questions include: "What are the facts?" "What assumptions am I making?" "What do others think, feel, and want?" "What's possible?" "What's best to do now?" This more thoughtful approach envisions solutions where everyone can discover, grow, and succeed. It's the route Michael took to try to repair his marriage. And it's the path Jim Weddle took when faced with the challenge from his employee. Weddle listened, expanded his viewpoint, and eventually made his organization better for everyone.[2]

Courage

As the section above suggests, courage plays a critical role in curiosity. But it's not your traditional manly courage.

Men grow up knowing we should be daring. Ready to run into the burning building. Willing to bet big on a business venture that could bring us riches or leave us bankrupt. Prepared to give up our life for our country. Related to such sacrifices is a tradition of men taking a stance that demonstrates moral courage—such as protesting for civil rights or speaking up on behalf of a colleague who's been mistreated at work. While these kinds of courage are honorable and may at times be necessary, they're also limited in scope, and they're not your everyday experience.

This second C concerns a much wider application and expression of courage. This bravery extends beyond physical, financial, and ethical matters. It includes the courage to confront suffering in ourselves and others, to change our beliefs, and to experience strong emotion. This courage is the fortitude to enter the uncharted territory of deep self-reflection and the landscape of feelings—including empathy and compassion for others. It also includes curiosity and being willing to give up the need for complete control—and instead to trust in the possibilities of collaborating and creating with others.

These additional kinds of valor, this personal courage, means standing up from the fearful crouch that so many confined men are stuck in. It's a man having the audacity to open his arms wide, to embrace others, and to open his heart to the joys, yearnings, and sorrows he and those around him feel. After all, the root of "courage" is "cor"—Latin for "heart."

Why is this bigger definition of courage, including emotional courage, important for moving toward liberating masculinity? Because men have to uncover and confront deep-seated, reactive fears if they are to break free of confined masculinity. Fears about being inadequate and unmanly in our own eyes, as well as in the eyes of others. Fears about losing status. Fears about trusting others, since confined men tend to view people with suspicion. Facing these fears is crucial to cultivating greater honesty with ourselves and stronger connections to others. In turn, the resulting authenticity, greater self-awareness, and robust bonds give life more meaning. They're also increasingly vital to success in our personal relationships and in our work lives—and to the well-being of our shrinking planet.

What does this broader courage look like in action? Think back to John, whose story we shared in the introduction. John felt deeply unhappy and lonely: his marriage was stale, his work was stressful—and alcohol and sex were proving to be empty fixes. But rather than remain in his misery, John chose to take the plunge into his own psyche in therapy with Ed Adams. It was scary. But he let his guard down in order to "let my truth out."

As John opened up, he learned to trust Ed. And as he allowed himself to be vulnerable, he was able to build relationships with other men. John realized he wasn't alone. His resilience improved—to the point where he could weather a divorce— and his life expanded, thanks to the personal, emotional courage he dared to demonstrate.

Stirring examples of emotional courage can be found among famous men as well. Consider the actor Brad Pitt. Pitt portrayed hyper-masculine male characters in a number of films, including the alpha-male alter ego to Edward Norton's mild-mannered man in the 1999 film *Fight Club*.

Pitt's own conception of manhood had much in common with those portrayals of confined masculinity. "I grew up with that be-capable, be-strong, don't-show-weakness thing," Pitt told the *New York Times*.

And yet that version of masculinity did not seem to serve Pitt in real life. His marriage to actress Angelina Jolie collapsed, reportedly related to his drinking problem. Pitt then spent a year and a half in Alcoholics Anonymous with a recovery group composed entirely of men. And just as John found comfort and camaraderie in an M3 group, Pitt gained a great deal in his de facto men's group.

Pitt shared much of himself with the other men, and they honored his trust. No one from the group told Pitt's stories to tabloid publications—which would have paid plenty for them.

"You had all these men sitting around being open and honest in a way I have never heard," Pitt told the *New York Times*. "It was actually really freeing just to expose the ugly sides of yourself."

In the *New York Times* profile, Pitt took the measure of

a traditional, constrained masculinity. Though he appreciated its attention to competency and self-sufficiency, he also pointed to its significant limitations.

"I'm grateful that there was such an emphasis on being capable and doing things on your own with humility, but what's lacking about that is taking inventory of yourself," he said. "It's almost a denial of this other part of you that is weak and goes through self-doubts, even though those are human things we all experience. Certainly, it's my belief that you can't really know yourself until you identify and accept those things."[3]

Pitt's vulnerability with his AA group and his introspection took guts. The courage needed to move toward liberating masculinity involves a willingness to look hard in the mirror and see all of ourselves—warts, weaknesses, everything.

There's a paradoxical power in this kind of courage. According to the rules of confined masculinity, trusting others and admitting one's flaws are sucker moves. But openness and authenticity arc actually sources of profound strength. In one of the most-viewed TEDx talks, scholar Brené Brown upended conventional wisdom about vulnerability. "Vulnerability sounds like truth and feels like courage," Brown says. "Truth and courage aren't always comfortable, but they're never weakness."[4]

To practice this kind of courage—to face fundamental fears and truly open our hearts—men can draw from a well-spring of mettle. We can build on the bravery we've been taught to embody from an early age. We can take a deep breath and let our truth out, as John did. We can take a leap of faith in others, as both John and Brad Pitt did. And like Pitt, we can face our full selves and accept our human weaknesses.

Odds are, we'll grow stronger, and our hearts will swell.

Compassion

The third C—compassion—is about opening the hearts of men. Compassion is about men letting their hearts be touched—and even broken—by suffering, and then working to relieve that suffering or prevent it in the first place. The anguish can range from physical pain to emotional grief to spiritual sorrow. Compassion applied to self and others requires empathy, but it doesn't stop there. It includes taking action.

We're talking about being compassionate with ourselves when we fail to reach a goal, or experience the death of a loved one. We're talking about extending care to a friend battling cancer, to a teenage child experiencing their first heartbreak, to a stranger struggling to make ends meet.

There is a courage piece to this too. It is painful to truly witness the pain of others. Confined masculinity trains us to steer clear of emotions, to remain stoic. So we often react to suffering with caution, indifference, avoidance, or even anger. Anger in many cases is a mask for fear and sadness. It takes courage to take that mask off, to confront fear and experience difficult emotions.

Jerry, mentioned earlier in the book, wrestled with expressing true compassion. Jerry gained a fuller life through self-reflection, which encouraged him to leave a toxic workplace and become a leader in M3. But long before that, when he first started attending M3 meetings, Jerry had reacted to men's tales of trouble and distress by saying things like, "Don't worry, it'll be okay," and "You're going to turn out fine."

Though these hopeful proclamations were well intentioned, they prevented Jerry from going to the dark place that his fellow M3 members were describing. Jerry's platitudes got in the way of other men being fully heard. They cut off genuine compassion.

Jerry's experience isn't unique. Confronting suffering evokes anxiety, and anxiety will almost always tell you to avoid the thing you fear. In their therapy sessions, Ed began calling Jerry's attention to this habit. And in time Jerry changed. In his role as M3 group leader, he now shows the emotional courage to deeply listen to and be with any man's difficulties. Jerry's leadership has become an act of deep compassion—for him, compassion and leadership are inseparable.

Why is compassion vital to a reinvented masculinity? Because it expands our life in multiple, positive ways. It enables us to "grow down"—that is, by being kind to ourselves we can develop a richer interior life of self-awareness and self-acceptance. Compassion also allows us to be better men to the people and other living creatures surrounding us. We become more empathetic spouses, fathers, and friends. And compassion is more and more critical to effectiveness at work, as well as to our survival as a human race.

How do you practice compassion? The short answer: with your head, heart, and hands. Start by believing compassion is central to masculinity. Identify and be willing to witness your own suffering as well as that of others. Then take action to ease the suffering. Or, if that is a struggle for you, you can also go the opposite route. Prod yourself to act with self-compassion and compassion toward others who suffer. Your behaviors can trigger new emotions, beliefs, and outcomes.

Take the case of Nathan, described in the liberating masculinity chapter. The experience of giving roses to hospital patients opened his eyes to the trials of others. It also widened his emotional landscape, and lifted his own spirits in the bargain. In effect, the work of his hands expanded his mind and opened his heart.

For another example of a compassionate man, consider coauthor Ed Frauenheim's teenage son Julius. Not long ago, Ed was driving his family home to San Francisco from Arizona and took a wrong turn at the famous "Grapevine" just north of Los Angeles. Ed yelled in frustration. His fury was partly about the time that would be lost, and partly about the shame of making a "stupid" mistake. This was a prime example of how men can cover up embarrassment and disappointment with anger.

Julius saw right through the explosive outburst.

"Dad, everything you are is already enough," he said calmly from the back seat.

Julius's words immediately eased Ed's mind. They got to the heart of the matter—and they healed Ed's momentary heartache.

Julius's simple act of compassion was in keeping with the way he and many young men are learning to incorporate kindness and empathy into their masculine ethos.[5] Julius was fortunate enough to learn conflict-resolution skills in elementary school, which is part of a wider trend where children are being taught "social-emotional learning" capabilities such as self-awareness, self-management, social awareness, relationship skills, and responsible decision-making.[6] It's a hopeful trend.

Confined masculinity tends to view compassion as unmanly, as "touchy-feely," as "soft." But this view of compassion has it backward. The "soft" stuff leads to strong business results, men in touch with their feelings are happier, and compassion is the birthright of every man.

Ed Adams has a bumper sticker on his car that reads, COMPASSIONATE MEN ARE HAPPIER. Drivers behind him often beep their horn with a "thumbs-up" to that message.

We can and must reinstate compassion as a masculine trait—for our own benefit and for the good of everyone around us.

Connection

"The good of everyone around us."

This phrase speaks to the fourth C: connection. Connection means men building stronger bonds with others and putting themselves more fully in service of people and planet. These deeper relationships involve recognizing our interdependence as a species and the fact that we are hardwired to connect with others.

Connection means fathers developing close, emotionally honest bonds with sons and daughters. This is about men seeing themselves as brothers to men and women of all backgrounds, races, and nationalities. We're calling for men to widen their circle of care and to behave as stewards of life on earth.

Why is connection important? Simply put, it is liberating

and powerful. How can bonds with others be freeing? This is a freedom that comes *with* others. This liberty stems from our fundamentally social nature as primates and human beings. It includes liberation from loneliness as well as the way others can unlock the best in us.

Another advantage of connection is power. The power to do with others what we can't do alone. The ability to create with others what we can't generate on our own. The excitement and impact of being part of something that is bigger than ourselves.

What's more, the liberation and power of connection are only growing more important. Strong bonds and a sense of our profound mutuality are proving to be increasingly vital in all aspects of our lives.

What does connection look like in practice? Similar to compassion, connection involves cultivating the right mindset, the right "heartset," and the right set of hands. That is, it calls for building certain beliefs such as trust, opening your heart to yourself and others, and developing habits that increase our connection with others.

For a good example, consider the way Raúl Ramos fathers his two teenage sons. Raúl, one of Ed Frauenheim's best friends, is a history professor at the University of Houston. He's active in the life of the university, and recently served as president of the faculty senate. But Raúl has never let his professional life overshadow his connection with his sons Joaquin and Noe. He has demonstrated his devotion to the boys by sharing childcare and household chore duties with his wife, Liz. He has served as a PTA board member of the boys' elementary school. He has also supported his kids as athletes, spending many hours practicing sports with Noe and Joaquin, finding the right baseball and lacrosse teams for his sons, and cheering them on.

This isn't to say he's a saint of a father. He yells at his boys occasionally. And he's not a perfect role model when it comes to his own fitness—he misses his monthly running goal more often than he hits it. In these ways, he's like a lot of dads. But Raúl stands out for being emotionally attuned to his kids.

Not long ago, Ed and Raúl were at a skate park in San Francisco while Julius, Joaquin, and Noe skateboarded. Raúl surprised Ed by correctly predicting that Joaquin would try to skate up a particular ramp, using a particular trick, even though Joaquin was halfway across the park at the time. Raúl also correctly predicted that Joaquin wouldn't quite pull off the trick—of reaching the top of the ramp on his board—and would instead grab onto a fence and let his skateboard slide back down. The board then posed a risk to other skaters.

"Hey, Joaquin, don't let your board loose like that," Raúl called out.

He reprimanded Joaquin, but not harshly. Through his habit of watching Joaquin closely, Raúl understood how much his son wanted to master the trick. Partly as a result of this kind of attentive, caring parenting, Joaquin is growing up as a kid who pours himself into his passions. He is a skilled catcher in baseball, a talented pianist, and fluent in both English and Spanish—with a bit of Chinese thrown in. Not bad for a ninth grader.

There's another facet of Raúl's father-son bonds. Joaquin and Noe are multiracial kids growing up in an ever-more-complex racial, socio-economic milieu. Raúl is a second-generation Latino and Liz is Chinese American. They live in Houston, which is both an inclusive, cosmopolitan community and a city with persistent racial divides. One incident highlights this complicated landscape of identity. A Latino player on the Houston Astros professional baseball team demeaned an Asian player on a rival team with a racist gesture—making "slant eyes." It was a confusing moment for Raúl's sons—being both Latino and Asian. But Raúl was there to speak with them about it.

Some may say Raúl's parenting has come at a cost. It's true he has delayed scholarly articles and books he is interested in developing. And he might have advanced further in his profession by now if he'd been a less-devoted dad. But Raúl does not regret the connections he's built with his kids. In other words, he doesn't wish he'd loved them less.

"I don't feel I'm paying a price, because I'm gaining so much," he says. "This is so much more important."

Unlike Raúl, generations of confined men have withheld affection from their children. Many of Ed Adams's patients are men who are sad that they are strangers to their own sons and daughters. But men can rebel against the misguided man-rules of stoicism and detachment. They can express love to their family members more fully—and they can extend positive connections to friends, colleagues, and the whole human family.

Commitment

Confined masculinity, despite being dangerously outdated, has significant cultural clout that's hard to escape. And so the fifth C, commitment, is a bit different than the first four. It acknowledges the fact that men can slip back to a confined masculinity—and resolves to prevent that from happening. It's about persevering in building habits of curiosity, courage, compassion, and connection. It's about determination to keep moving in the direction of liberating masculinity.

When men are committed to reinventing their masculinity, they enjoy remarkable rewards. They experience the liberation and power we've explored throughout the book. They enjoy greater happiness and a deeper involvement with life. So, how do you make a commitment to liberating masculinity?

As with the other Cs, commitment involves head, heart, and hands. It requires belief, passion, and behavior change, all in the service of a better, more fulfilling way to be a man.

Commitment begins with understanding that you are making a commitment to move away from a style of masculinity that often diminishes experiences in life rather than enhancing them. So committing to travel the liberating masculinity path makes rational sense.

One vehicle that many liberating men use to go down that path is meditation, sometimes combined with yoga. Meditation, also known as mindfulness, is directly aligned with the goals of increasing compassion and connection. Coauthor Ed Frauenheim credits a regular yoga practice over two decades with helping him stay devoted to becoming a stronger, kinder, calmer man.

What's more, there is a science to self-improvement. Men can benefit from the insights of behavioral economics, which suggests nudges and small changes to routines in order to build up positive habits. Men also can take advantage of digital tools to keep them on track. They can use mindfulness and happiness apps to prompt them to demonstrate kindness. They can set up calendar items to remind them to ask more questions. They can arrange to expand their information sources to get news about different cultures and points of view to foster more compassion and greater connection.

Men today are gravitating to personal data analytics to improve their athletic performance or overall health. They can harness some of the same principles and technologies to update and enhance their masculinity.

Even with the right tips and tools, though, inspiration helps. Along these lines, consider this story about a man who persisted in practicing a compassionate and connected kind of masculinity.

Tony Bond is chief diversity and innovation officer at Great Place to Work, the research and consulting firm where coauthor Ed Frauenheim also works.

Tony's father was a construction worker who became disabled with silicosis, a work-related lung disease, when Tony was just one year old. Despite the ailment and physical weakness, Tony remembers his dad as a gentle, generous spirit. "He instilled in me the need to listen more than you talk," Tony recalls. "To be present for people."

Tony's father and mother also taught him important lessons about character and quiet strength by how they reacted to racial slurs and insensitivity. His dad was mixed-race, with some African American ancestry. His mother was part African American, part Native American. Growing up, Tony witnessed the two rise above racist remarks and rude stares.

Tony carried values of humility and dignity to college, and eventually to the work world. During his early years in corporate finance and sales, though, Tony's way of being a man wasn't always appreciated. He recalls how competing for attention and seeking to dominate conversations were common among his peers. "The louder you can be, the more you can say, the more aggressive you can show up, the more you're valued, and the more you're recognized," Tony says. "I found this tension between who I am and what I was expected to be."

Things came to a head at a sales strategy meeting. Tony had his own ideas on how to proceed and mostly listened, trying to learn from the usual combative conversation. In the wake of the meeting, he was criticized for being passive and "quiet." So he spoke to a vice president he respected. "I remember him saying, 'You're in this for the long run. Results speak for themselves. And don't feel like you have to change,'" Tony says. "That's when I dug my heels in and said, 'I don't really care what the expectation is. I'm just going to be who I am.'"

Tony also sought out others who shared his view that better treatment of people mattered. Eventually he discovered Great Place to Work, which studies and celebrates organizations where leaders emphasize respect, credibility, and fairness.

Ironically, Tony's hunt for an organization that values listening has given him a loud voice. At Great Place to Work, he criss-crosses the globe speaking with business executives and giving talks about innovation, diversity, and the future of work.[7] One key to this happy ending was Tony's ability to persist in being someone with a "me and we" orientation. Another was finding an organization that made room for a man determined to remain curious and focused on connecting with others.

About Great Place to Work, he says, "I never really felt like I had to show up with that macho bravado. You could take the uniform and the mask off, and be who you are."

He adds: "I found it liberating."

The Combination of the Five Cs

The Five Cs are a set of ingredients to mix together to reinvent a man's masculine identity. Or, think of them as destinations that are part of a larger quest. They all are vital, like challenges in a video game that result in items needed for the larger, final test. But the Five Cs do not have to be worked in a particular order. Any of them can serve as the entry point for beginning the transformation to liberating masculinity.

The Five Cs overlap and interrelate with each other. Curiosity is inherently courageous. Courage touches on compassion, and vice versa. Connection relies heavily on the first three Cs. Curiosity invites us to ask about ways we are interconnected. Courage is required to push back against the confined masculinity mandate to be an isolated, self-sufficient island. Compassion can fuel connection, as a man's heart is stirred into action by a living creature in need.

The Five Cs are also recurring. They are cyclical. Men on the path to liberating masculinity will keep working on these five practices, moving through them again and again. Eventually, they will sink deeply into his bones. But there is never a precise finish line. A man can always keep expanding his awareness and his heart.

While all the Five Cs are essential, two are central to the freedom and power that comes from reinventing your masculinity: compassion and connection. We explore each of these in greater detail in the chapters ahead.

THINGS TO PONDER AND DO

CURIOSITY: Let your imagination run wild. Start a journal in which you ask a new question every day. Include open-ended questions, especially ones that challenge your assumptions about manhood. Don't judge or censor your thoughts.

Over time, do you notice how traditional, confined views of masculinity have shaped your life?

Also, write about the man you want to be.

COURAGE: Share with someone what makes you most afraid and what brings you the deepest joy.

Can you step up and demonstrate courage by taking a stand against injustice? You can write a letter to the editor or refuse to participate in conversations that denigrate others.

Recognize that you're being courageous when you break free of the harmful and limiting rules of confined masculinity. Challenge yourself by taking emotional risks with a friend or colleague. And if there is someone you've mistreated by following the rules of confined masculinity, find the courage to apologize.

COMPASSION: Start with self-compassion. Think of a hurt you experienced in the past, or perhaps still feel. Can you move more deeply into that pain? Then, reassure yourself of your resilience and ability to learn from that hurt. Be kind and forgiving to yourself.

Think of someone you know who is suffering. Tell them that you are sincerely concerned about them, and listen to their story. Then do something tangible to help relieve their discomfort.

Follow Nathan's compassionate footsteps: bring a dozen roses to a hospital and give one to each patient who seems to be all alone.

CONNECTION: Consider which of your personal relationships you most want to deepen. How can you begin to build a more heart-centered bond with that person?

Join a men's support group, or attend a workshop intended to encourage men to confront and share life experiences.

Ask yourself: how can you live in a way that is more connected to the earth? What small steps can you take that will make you a better steward of the planet?

COMMITMENT: Get a base-level measurement of where you fall on the continuum from confined masculinity to liberating masculinity. Take the Reinventing Masculinity Self-Assessment (found at ReinventingMasculinity.com and at the end of the book). Track your progress by retaking the assessment every six months.

Create a challenging self-query like, "What kind of man do I want to be in this moment?" and remind yourself: "I am unique but not the most important person in this room." Come back to your question and to this statement throughout the day.

Gift of Compassion

4   The Liberating Power of Compassion

Ed Adams asked his wife, "Is this room tilted?" "No," she said. "Why do you ask?" That question turned out to be the opening salvo of a health saga that put him in the hospital for two weeks as his body slowly become paralyzed from the top down. As the symptoms progressed, the specter of death became a more and more likely outcome to the nightmare—made worse by the fact that no one knew what was happening to him.

Eventually, the diagnosis was found to be a rare immune disorder called Miller Fisher syndrome, which has an incidence of just one in a million. It's thought to be triggered by a virus that tricks the immune system into attacking its own neural system as if it were a foreign agent. Slowly the nervous system shorts out and body functions go haywire. That's the bad news. The good news is…it eventually stops. After it runs its destructive path, neurons begin to repair themselves. Eventually, normalcy returns; it's a trip to hell and back.

Ed's medical drama, a very frightening time that forced a reckoning with death, is now a decade-old memory. But despite the fear and anxiety he went through, Ed's recollection today doesn't center on the confusion, helplessness, and distress. Instead Ed remembers the compassion.

Suffering arouses compassion. Compassion is sensitivity to the suffering in self and others with a commitment to try to alleviate and prevent it. In his round-trip flight on the Miller Fisher syndrome journey, Ed's suffering evoked compassion from countless numbers of people. Physicians, nurses (especially the nurses), technicians, other patients, his wife, family, and friends. He was on the receiving end of a river of compassion. One friend joked with Ed about his inability to articulate words clearly, quipping: "You don't need to talk much to do therapy with men, Ed. They don't listen to you anyway." He laughed when Ed could only grunt.

Throughout the two weeks in the hospital, one dose of Tylenol was the only medication Ed took. He states with full confidence that it was the compassion he received that "healed my spirit." Ed hears echoes of the power of compassion in the myriad stories told by people affected by the COVID-19 pandemic.

Compassion is a natural expression of our human nature that all men need in order to live healthy, satisfying, soulful lives. But, in addition to being willing to give and receive compassion, men need to be compassionate with themselves as well. Compassion and its cousin behaviors—empathy, kindness, self-awareness, appreciation, and generosity—have always been central to deeply rewarding relationships for men. Yet today acting with a compassionate mindset has become imperative. Changes in technology, demographics, and organizational life are putting a premium on emotional awareness when it comes to men's personal happiness, their effectiveness at work, and their place in our wider society. Compassion and self-compassion are liberating men from a "me"-only self-centeredness that generates unnecessary suffering and isolation. The compassion at the heart of liberating masculinity is enabling men to manage a more complex, relationship-centered world in meaningful, powerful ways.

A Human Hallmark, a Man's Birthright

Humans have evolved with the ability to intimately connect with our children, an ability that ensured newborns received the care needed to survive. Fortunately, the capacity to form bonds with others extends beyond our immediate family. If our early ancestors hadn't take care of each other, our clans would have perished. We learned that mutual attention and care makes us better able to not just survive but also to thrive. It becomes a two-way emotional payoff: we can experience the comfort of receiving compassion and feel satisfaction providing it.

Consider how compassion scholar Paul Gilbert sums up our early history as a species.

"With the advent of agriculture, peaceful and caring hunter-gatherer bands that had existed for hundreds of thousands of years fragmented. It was in these groups, however, that we evolved the extraordinary capacity for empathy, caring, and sharing," Gilbert says. "In fact, it's likely that human intelligence and language evolved partly *because* we focused on developing prosocial relationships."[1]

Compassion itself has no gender boundaries. Emma

Seppälä, science director of the Stanford Center for Compassion and Altruism Research and Education, argues it is misguided to view women as being more innately compassionate than men. "While women's expression involved nurturing and bonding," Seppälä writes, "men's compassion was expressed through protecting and ensuring survival. Compassion just took on a different 'look and feel' depending on our evolutionary needs for survival."[2] And so, if men claim that compassion is exclusively a feminine trait, they deny themselves their full humanity.

Compassion originates in our nature and is positively or negatively shaped by experience. Since compassion is integrated into our humanity, it's like an acorn waiting to be developed—or not. Everyone is born with the need and capacity to be connected to others. Environmental experiences that begin in utero and extend throughout life continuously shape our access to and expression of our compassionate selves. All of us are capable of great heights or lows, of developing the compassion of Buddha or the callous indifference of a psychopath.

Men are by both nature and nurture compassionate beings. Confined masculinity, though, can hold men back from identifying compassion as a trait to be valued and nurtured. Men have often disavowed kindness, tenderness, and caring as being "masculine" because these traits have been perceived as soft and feminine—and we know that confined masculinity marginalizes that which is perceived as feminine. But we need to understand that compassion must be fully claimed into the humanity of men. The time has come for men to reclaim compassion as masculine, to bring it back into male identity. Reclaiming compassion and self-compassion energizes the soul of men. It is also required for positive and sustainable change in the world.

Ed Adams has treated a great number of men, who come to him to address any number of problems. And none of them has had the problem of "too much tenderness, care, and compassion" in his life.

A Father's Regret

Jackson, a member of Men Mentoring Men, illustrates how compassion or the lack thereof can have a significant impact on relationships.

After participating in a dozen men's group meetings and listening to the other men open up, Jackson decided to reveal what was locked in his heart. During one M3 meeting, he discussed the shame he felt about the way he fathered his young adult daughter, Sara.

"At the start I was disappointed that we had a girl," he admitted. "I tried to interest her in the things I enjoy like sports, camping, and fishing and anything that was competitive. But she wasn't interested in these things. Actually, she's more like a girlie girl. I made little effort to show interest in her activities. Sara experienced me as a distant and disconnected father. As I look back, I can see how much I hurt her. Naturally, we grew apart. Now I want to become closer to Sara and show her my love. But I'm scared it's too late. I don't know what to do."

Jackson began to understand that he had accepted and abided by many confined masculinity rules. One of these rules tells us that it's unmanly to act in ways that are stereotypically labeled as feminine. The problems Jackson faced were a consequence of following such antiquated and limiting ideas. As a result, Jackson was living in regret and disappointment. But Jackson is a loving man who was seeking the liberating power of compassion and connection.

The men at this meeting bore witness to Jackson's emotional pain. The room remained silent until Jackson continued. "I came to this group too late," he concluded. "If I had seen the world through the lens of compassion, life for my daughter and me would have worked out differently. I would have seen Sara's hurt and I would have helped her. I love her. Now, we're both wounded."

But the men didn't think it was too late. They urged Jackson to figure out a strategy to reconnect with Sara. And what Jackson did next was quite an inspiration. But before we tell you what he did, let's discuss other key aspects related to men and compassion—starting with self-compassion.

Men and Self-Compassion

In the M3 meeting room there is a sign that states, I NEVER BEAT MYSELF UP GENTLY. That comment speaks to the way many men lack self-compassion.

When a man offers himself compassion, he is willing to recognize his own pain, discomfort, disappointment, and suffering—and then attempt to comfort himself to relieve that pain. We are being self-compassionate when we treat ourselves with kindness, caring, and respect. Self-compassion originates in our thoughts and then is put into action by our behavior.

Ed Adams facilitates workshops for men. Whenever he introduces the notion of self-compassion, he is usually met with blank stares. Self-compassion is a concept few men have ever heard about. But when Ed asks men if they are self-critical or think negatively about themselves, everyone raises their hand. One man said it well: "No one ever sat me down and said that it's time to learn how to be your own best friend."

Self-compassion is one of the essential skills men need to move from confined masculinity toward liberating masculinity. And since self-compassion is a learned skill, men of all ages can develop or increase their practice of self-compassion. This is a good thing, since the ability to be self-compassionate dramatically increases our quality of life. Kristin Neff, a leading researcher and proponent of self-compassion, found that self-compassion is more constructive to our psychological well-being than self-esteem. Self-esteem is judgment-based in that we compare ourselves to others; self-compassion, on the other hand, involves confronting realities of life but without unjustified or harsh judgment. Self-compassion refers to how we relate to ourselves about past, present, and anticipated experiences. "Self-compassion," Neff says, "is associated with greater emotional resilience, more accurate self-concepts, more caring relationship behavior, as well as less narcissism and reactive anger."[3]

Note that self-compassion is not a sugarcoated, trite way of thinking, such as "everything works out for the best" or "don't worry about it." Self-compassion is pragmatic and kind. It is based in the full-spectrum realities of life, the good, the bad, and the ugly. For example, one of Ed's patients was recently diagnosed with Parkinson's disease. If Ed told him that self-compassion was believing "it will work out in the end," Ed would both harm him and diminish the trust built between them within the therapeutic relationship. Instead, Ed suggested that he tell himself, "Parkinson's is surely going to make life difficult. But the good news is I am loved, supported, resilient, and aware. I am surrounded by people who care about me and a team of doctors committed to help me physically and emotionally cope with this disease."

Criticizing Self-Criticism

Harsh self-criticism cultivates feelings of being inadequate, "different," and "left out." These beliefs increase isolation, anxiety, and depression. The benefits of developing self-compassion include reducing fear and anxiety, as well as developing greater connection with others and stronger resilience to life stressors. Being compassionate toward yourself is practicing self-kindness. It helps regulate negative emotions by being a soothing source of self-comfort. It also allows a man stuck in a "me" orientation to open his interior life and all of his relationships to a more effective "me and we" worldview. One of the most destructive elements within confined masculinity is the notion that men should not express feelings, needs, emotions, or personal matters to anyone, even to oneself. As a consequence, self-compassion is impeded by the lack of language to identify and validate what is experienced. Ronald F. Levant, a leading researcher in men's studies, saw the inability to describe feelings with words so pervasive among men that he coined an academic term to capture the phenomenon: "normative male alexithymia."[4]

Although most men take pride in attending to the needs of their external life, ignoring one's inner landscape is one of the numerous drawbacks of a confined masculinity. Because without self-awareness—and the language to describe what one feels—men are susceptible to being misunderstood, dismissed, and relationally handicapped, all of which renders emotional growth stagnant or impossible. In addition, reluctance to identify and express emotion perpetuates the stereotype that talking about feelings isn't masculine. Often, the ability to recognize inner emotions is never learned because there was no one to teach it. This runs the risk of transmitting self-ignorance generation after generation—until some brave soul decides to venture inward. If a man is to enjoy the benefits of self-compassion, he must be aware of, accept, and describe what he really feels. He must understand the "feeling inside the feeling," the deeper emotion underneath the initial reaction to any unpleasant scenario.

In short, this is about developing emotional maturity and sophistication.

It may seem that men are becoming more expressive through the use of communication technologies—we've seen guys zapping smiley faces, hearts, and tearful emojis in their tweets and texts. But this effusiveness may not carry over to expressed emotion with someone facing you eye to eye. In other words, be aware that confined masculinity is an insidious, durable, and powerful force.

There is one emotion many men frequently access and express: anger. Anger is an emotional energy that can be directed to build relationships and create positive change. One can argue that Mother Teresa used anger to ensure that the poor, destitute, and sick under her care were not ignored. Anger is also an emotion that's perceived by many as "manly." But it's a dangerous emotion, and we caution against identifying it as a welcomed manly trait. Anger often is used as justification for violence and aggression. It is frequently "me" oriented and judgmental. Often, anger sickens the mind, alienates others and destroys relationships. There is no virtue in that outcome.

Anger often derives from self-absorption, from holding on to righteous positions. At M3 meetings, when participants don't agree with another man's point of view, Ed Adams has asked them to respond not with anger but with: "you might be right." This opens the conversation to discuss substance instead of defending positions. Those four words help to curb or even prevent anger responses.

Marty, one of Ed's patients, told him, "I was given a surprise party to celebrate my fortieth birthday. Instead of feeling honored, I was angry. Then, a guy at work teased me. Instead of laughing at myself, I became angry. Why so much anger? You're the doctor," he said to Ed. "Am I just an angry man?"

Men and Compassion

The answer to Marty's question is both yes and no. Yes, men living according to confined masculinity have been angry. But no, that isn't our natural state.

As we said, compassion and self-compassion are genderless. But when men associate compassionate thought and action as being soft, weak, or feminine, they're not likely to adopt compassion in their lives. In the liberating masculinity

Dawn

At 4:00 am every work day, Isaac drags himself out of bed. He goes to an unfulfilling job that provides income for food, shelter, and education for his wife and children. This means that when the alarm clock screams out, Isaac begins his day "doing what a man has to do."

But isn't manliness more than that? Could Isaac see his self-sacrifice as love? Could he affirm his own generosity and kindness? Could he identify himself as a compassionate man?

I ask because it truly matters, and Isaac needs to know.

—E. M. ADAMS

model, men proudly and eagerly associate compassion and self-compassion as manly. This deep connection between masculinity and compassion releases men to express their full humanity, and honors the selfless deeds many men perform every day. Compassion and self-compassion liberate men from self-centered anger; they also enable mindfulness. Mindfulness, in turn, allows the brain to self-regulate, and respond to incidents with a range of options.

Compassion is like a big container filled with the best of the human spirit. Once compassion is present within our mind and heart, it brings along empathy, connection, care, involvement, and "me and we" thinking—plus the positive action to fulfill those positive intentions. It is a highly virtuous characteristic of our humanity because it benefits both the self and others.

If the mythical magician Merlin waved his magic wand

and ignited a twofold greater presence of compassion within all human beings, problems from the individual to the global level would be positively affected enormously. The awareness of each other's needs and suffering would sharpen. Decisions would be informed by caring about the impact on self and others. Our connection to and responsibility for the welfare of the environment would not be in question. Wars and nuclear weapons would appear ludicrous. Famine and disease would be tackled in coordinated ways, no longer dominated by self-serving economic concerns. Each of us would feel that we are part of community and that our lives matter. We would experience greater purpose and live longer, healthier, and more satisfying lives. Given all these benefits of pursuing compassion-driven lives, it's folly for men not to accept compassion as a deeply manly quality.

The Ingredients of Compassion

Along with self-awareness and the ability to express our inner feelings, compassion extends out and requires caring about our relationships as well. For most people, the key relationships include immediate family, extended family, and perhaps some friends, colleagues, and even family pets. This is a circumscribed circle of relationship, which in turn generates a limited circle of compassion. This isn't to say that compassion at this level isn't vital and honorable. Most men who identify themselves as compassionate are responsive to those within their contained circle of relationships.

In the past, the expression of compassion toward those within this circle was adequate to survive and thrive. That is

Peace, Compassion, Death, and Life

Recently, Ed Adams was on a flight traveling cross-country. When he found his assigned seat, it was already occupied by a man who was comfortably settled in. They decided to just trade seats, which turned out to be a fortuitus decision.

In the new seat, Ed was next to a man named Carl. He was traveling to attend to his father, who had suddenly become very ill. The woman in the seat next to Carl was a kind and delightful businessperson named Shanti. She told them that she came from a Hindu tradition and that her name means "peace."

Midway through the six-hour flight, Carl learned that his father had passed away. He was heartbroken and filled with conflicting emotions. But by this time Carl knew that Ed was a psychologist writing a book about men and compassion, so he felt safe to talk to Ed—and Shanti—about his relationship with his father. He also felt a need to cry, but was constrained by the circumstances.

Ed suggested that Carl be mindful of ways he may feel the presence of his father, as well as ways he could express his love. Carl nodded and turned thoughtful. After a long silence, Carl nudged Ed and said, "I think my dad is talking to me. He put the two of you next to me to tell me that I need to live my life surrounded by peace and compassion."

no longer the case. Technology, communication, and transportation have made the world small. Our technological advancements have altered and expanded all relationships—to the extent that in today's world it's a challenge to effectively maintain our close contained relationships. In addition, many of our familial relationships are dispersing because of increased mobility, divorce, changing modes of communication, and economic and social changes.

Herein lies a paradox. Technology broadens our ability to witness the suffering of others but can diminish our ability to see it in those closest to us. For example, if my relationship with my nephew is based on short, shallow text messages, I may know nothing of his pain. I may not know if he has a broken heart, or wasn't promoted as he'd hoped. And yet, I can go online and witness the pain of people who lost everything in a fire. I might feel bad for that family without realizing my own nephew needs my attention and care. Instant communication can connect us with the suffering of others. Yet our current tools can nudge us toward superficial exchanges rather than real intimacy with those nearest to us.

Many of us around the globe are struggling with this paradox. This makes it urgent for men to embrace compassion as a birthright of manhood. Only then can we deal with the confusion that hovers around compassion—and the difficulty of enacting it in our close relationships and then amplifying it to reach others.

Compassion also is emerging as a critical behavior for successful careers and thriving organizations. We'll explore this idea in greater detail in chapter six, "Reinventing Masculinity at Work." The gist, though, is that a quicker, more complex, more diverse business world is calling for both men and women to demonstrate emotional intelligence, empathy, and caring. These soft skills are proving to also be "success skills," since persuasion is becoming more powerful than top-down commands, organizations rely increasingly on teams rather than individual efforts, and "psychological safety" among colleagues is critical.

Men living within a liberating masculinity model are comfortable with kindness, and they often thrive in the new business climate. But the men who remain stoic and uninterested in understanding the experience of historically marginalized people, such as women, people of color, and LGBTQ colleagues, are finding themselves less and less effective. They also face greater risk of violating the higher standards of sensitivity that organizations are adopting.

An Always-Available Option

But there's hope for these men to move in the right direction. Compassion is always available. We have the omnipresent choice to respond to life in this way. Ed Adams's cross-country flight (see the "Peace, Compassion, Death, and Life" sidebar) demonstrated how compassion and kindness can be chosen over indifference. Compassion is a highly effective antidote to contained masculinity. Expanding and compassionate men express feelings, ask questions, reveal needs and desires, and enter difficult conversations with the intent to resolve conflict, not increase it.

In liberating masculinity, character matters. A man is measured by his intention and willingness to create harmony and cooperate with others. Empathy, kindness, appreciation, and respect are prized characteristics. A liberating man highly values compassion, and integrates it into every action and decision at every level in his personal and organizational lives. A compassionate man knows that "what goes around, comes around." This acknowledges that all life interconnects—and if you act with compassion and kindness, you will soon be the beneficiary of those traits. Likewise, if each of us acts with detachment and in a "me" orientation, eventually our own needs will be ignored by others.

Compassion is a virtuous behavior. Ed Adams invariably advises men in the throes of divorce to respond to the hurt and anger by "taking the high ground." One of his patients, Wade, was going through a nightmare divorce filled with accusation, legal maneuvers, and threats to his business. Despite his many fears, Wade tried hard to control his impulses to respond with anger. "I hate what my wife is doing," he told Ed, "but I refuse to hate her."

Throughout Wade's ordeal, Ed and Wade discussed the pros and cons of responding to his ex-wife with strength and compassion. Wade discovered that it takes a great deal of courage to maintain a more peaceful course. He also learned that he could set firm boundaries, and learned the value of self-compassion.

After the dust settled and both parties moved on with their lives, Wade reflected on the difficult divorce. "As I look back, I am so happy that I generally kept true to my moral compass. I lost money but not my kids, and I lost some battles but I kept my integrity. Now, I'm scarred, but open to loving and being loved."

He emerged from his trouble with his fatherhood intact, and he became a wiser and more connected man. Compassion and self-compassion guided his journey toward an expansion of his masculinity rather than a retreat toward a constrained, "me"-centered, crouching stance.

Courageous Compassion

Compassion is not for the faint of heart. It calls for a gritty, face-to-face acceptance of pain and suffering combined with genuine, realistic, kind, and bold responses. Compassionate men are not pincushions. They maintain healthy boundaries, even as they act to relieve and prevent suffering. They respond to compassion's call to act with curiosity, courage, connection, and a firm commitment to prevent, ease, and end suffering in ourselves and others.

These themes we've discussed above played a major role in how Jackson—mentioned earlier in the chapter—resolved his conflict with his daughter. You may recall Jackson's long-standing alienation from his daughter, Sara. Jackson expressed his desire to "improve" the relationship and said that he wanted to "become more connected and loving," but he also didn't know what to do. During the M3 meeting mentioned earlier, Jackson's helplessness was carefully challenged by the other men. Then total silence. Suddenly, Jackson stood up and asked if he could use Ed's private office to make a call.

Twenty minutes later, Jackson returned. "I called Sara," he announced to the men. "I told her I love her and I was so sorry for how unloving I acted toward her. I told her that things were going to be different and if she let me back into her life, I promised that I will do all I can to make our relationship work. Then we both cried. Sara said, 'I love you, dad.' And I told her that she was the love of my life."

All the men in the room applauded. Many were in tears.

When Ed Adams was in the hospital with Miller Fisher syndrome, his bodily functions shutting down, he was physically helpless. His mind, however, was working fine, so he could cognitively process all that was going on. He knew the medical staff was perplexed. The majority of his doctors had never seen or even heard of the syndrome. Throughout that helpless state of growing paralysis, the only thing Ed could rely on was the continuous compassion of everyone helping him.

It was compassion that saved his soul. Now, let it work its power on you.

THINGS TO PONDER AND DO

CURIOSITY: What evokes compassion in you? Can you identify male gender rules that suppress compassionate living?

COURAGE: Perform a compassionate act that takes you out of your comfort zone. How does this feel to you, and what impact does it have on the recipient of your compassion?

COMPASSION: Practice an act of self-compassion. Can you recognize a hurt you feel and consciously soothe yourself? It may help to share your pain with a friend.

CONNECTION: Reach out to someone who seems to be struggling. Be honest about the pain you see in them. Ask what you can do to ease their suffering.

COMMITMENT: At night when you're in bed, reflect on compassion before you fall asleep. Think back on the compassion you showed someone else recently, and be grateful for the compassion you've received.

One

5 The Liberating Power of Connection

"I don't mind solitude," Roy explained to Ed Adams during a therapy session. "I don't mind going to places like restaurants and movies by myself. But sometimes I feel so lonely I ache. And that, I do mind. As I think about it, one of my greatest fears is being unable to care for myself and dying alone."

An epidemic of loneliness exists in the United States, affecting millions of men and boys. The former U.S. Surgeon General Vivek Murthy called loneliness the most common threat to public health. In an article in the *Harvard Business Review*, Dr. Murthy stated that seclusion or "weak social connections, are associated with a reduction of lifespan similar to that caused by smoking fifteen cigarettes a day and even greater than that associated with obesity."[1]

It seems that loneliness actually increases our susceptibility to physical and emotional problems such as cardiovascular disease, dementia, depression, and anxiety. In 2005, the Australian Longitudinal Study of Ageing found that friendships increased life expectancy by as much as 22 percent. It turns out that friendships positively affect life extension even more than family relationships do.[2]

Loneliness also creates confusion for men. On the one hand, loneliness feels lousy. On the other hand, men aren't supposed to express pain, complain, or be needy. After all, a central value of confined masculinity is self-sufficiency—not needing anyone or anything else. Men like Roy silently suffer the pangs of loneliness while trying to convince themselves that loneliness doesn't matter. Roy not only feels lonely, but his quality of life is diminished. As the surgeon general suggested, friendships, companionship, and intimacy offer us great benefits. In poetic terms, connections give life wings.

And those wings matter more and more. In the twenty-first century, connection is vital for men to live a full life. Cultivating social ties and an awareness of our interdependence is increasingly important to men in their individual relationships, in their organizations, and in society. Connection frees men from loneliness and from a myopic perspective, and provides opportunities to grow down into deep understanding and intimacy with the world. Put simply, connection delivers the power to thrive at home, at work, and at play.

Suicidal Isolation

How can you play if you have no close pals to play with? In one of Ed's psychotherapy sessions with Roy, he asked Roy if he had a best friend. Roy replied, "I do. Stan. I've known Stan for twenty-five years. I see him once in a while, but we always talk to each other around New Year's. It's the kind of relationship where we always seem to pick up where we left off. I look forward to our annual call."

Sadly, Roy rarely got to interact with his best friend.

We are hardwired to connect. The need for human-to-human connection is woven into our hearts and minds. Connection transcends gender and is archetypal. Connection is present no matter what other tribal distinctions we impose upon others. Yet, somehow men often fail to comprehend this reality; instead, they perpetuate the belief that real men are independent and self-sufficient. The truth is that men who choose to separate themselves from others are performing acts of emotional suicide.

And when our culture encourages men to be stoic and less feeling, our culture assists in that suicide. In a society that possesses such great wealth and innovation, we pay little homage to our collective emotional needs, especially the skills to develop meaningful human connection. The set of beliefs of confined masculinity is one of the most powerful engines that drives that destructive ethos. It denies men the comfort that close and intimate connection provides.

Men could use that comfort. The proportion of men living alone in 2018 was twice what it was in 1970.[3] And the isolation of millions of men is leading to despair and death. One study found that middle-aged men who have many close relationships can weather three or more incidents of intense stress per year—such as divorce, financial trouble, or getting fired—without an increase in their mortality rate. That level of stress, though, tripled the death rate of socially isolated middle-aged men.[4] Simply put, confined masculinity is killing men. But

A Father's Faltering Friendships

Ed Frauenheim's father has suffered from confined masculinity when it comes to friendships. Ed shares that story:

While growing up in Buffalo, New York, I saw my dad enjoy a number of close friendships. Some dated to his childhood, like Peter and Claudia—who got married and lived down the street from us. But as my dad moved to different parts of the country to pursue his own new jobs or those of my mother, those friendships eroded.

By the time he was in his sixties, my dad treated my mom, Marty, as the only friend he needed. But the limits of my dad's few friendships became clear once my mom died in 2014. He described his life as a "void" without my mom. He moved to be near my brother in St. Paul, Minnesota, but hasn't expanded his social world much beyond his own three kids and one or two business partners. And he has wrestled with loneliness.

"I have lost, perhaps, the art of making new friends," my dad told me.

My dad has bucked some of the conventions of traditional masculinity in the course of his life. For example, he was willing to swap breadwinning and homemaker roles with my mom as her education career advanced. But after she died my dad reverted to equating his self-worth with the size of his bank account. And a lack of financial success in recent years—despite attempting to earn a living as a Lyft driver—has hindered him from connecting with old friends.

"I have had dreams where I was back with Peter and Claudia, and wondering how they're doing," he told me. "And at the same time, I've always been afraid that by getting in touch with them again I would be causing them grief, because they know how far I've fallen."

"In what sense, fallen?" I asked my dad.

"Without mom, without Mart, I'm very low on the economic scale. And my life is just nothing like it used to be. And I'm afraid that if I get into talking with people like Peter and Claudia, I am having to confess that that's my state in life."

The shame my father feels is rooted in part in a long-standing tenet of confined masculinity—be a provider and make a lot of money to prove your value. But that constraint has been exacerbated by economic and demographic changes. My dad now lives far from his old friends in Buffalo, making it easier for him to withdraw from them. And he's experiencing the difficulty of earning a decent, steady paycheck in our emerging "gig" economy. The result is another lonely, unhappy man. And a son saddened by his dad's suffering.

Note: At the request of Ed Frauenheim's father, the names of these friends have been changed.

since they're alone, their loneliness and isolation are often invisible.

Mental health professionals diagnose and treat men and women with various degrees of depression, anxiety, phobias, addictions, and destructive behaviors. Underlying these conditions is often abuse, lack of purpose, lack of belonging, fear of rejection and shame, or the belief that one is emotionally damaged. All of these conditions frequently share one essential ingredient: not being intimately connected with others in meaningful ways. This failure can occur in marriages, love relationships, friendships, and work settings. Unfortunately, disconnection is not restricted to our human relationships. We can become disconnected with other living creatures and the earth as well. Connection is not about sharing the same room, building, or planet. Connection happens when we look around and see and welcome our interdependence with all things.

Intimate Connections

In a TED talk in 2010, Dr. Brené Brown defined connection "as the energy that exists between people when they feel seen, heard, and valued; when they can give and receive without judgment; and when they derive sustenance and strength from the relationship."[5]

Intimacy with another person is one of life's most precious gifts. Yet, so many men fear, avoid, or hold back expressions of intimacy, or they depend upon sex to be the primary way to express it. When intimacy is narrowly defined, important emotional relationships will become truncated. And yet intimacy can be furthered with just a little time and effort.

Intimacy is a man hugging his spouse and whispering, "I love you," or a father getting down on the floor to play with his children. And when men share inner conflicts or confusions with other men, that's intimacy too.

Intimacy necessitates emotional vulnerability. But what important and creative act in life doesn't require some level of vulnerability? If you try a new recipe or attempt to change a tire, isn't there some risk of failure or inadequacy? Becoming more skilled at expressing intimacy requires courage and practice. But the men who move more deeply into intimacy by allowing themselves to be vulnerable soon find the rewards far exceed the risks. Intimate bonds create deep and satisfying connections that fill the painful voids within our hearts.

As noted earlier, intimate connections and human relationships are vital to greater life satisfaction, but intimate connections are not restricted to people. Most of us have witnessed or experienced the profoundly intimate bonds we can develop with our pets—and the powerful sadness and grief we can feel in losing them. This intimacy is created by shared experiences, mutual care, and many moments of physical touch. Animals not only crawl on our laps but move deeply into our hearts and imaginations. It's an intimacy that emerges out of trust, love, tenderness, and smiles. It hurts so much when we lose a source of intimate connection because connection touches our souls.

Connection to Nature

The story continues beyond our relationship with people and animals. Our connection with the earth is fundamental. If any

person or animal is to survive and thrive, then intimacy with
the earth is needed, and we must take care of it. When we
connect with the environment and understand our intimate
interdependence with nature, we become better caretakers of
our little planet. In turn, this increases the probability that the
planet will survive. But if we refuse to maintain intimacy with
the earth, that disconnection leads to collective suicide.

A confined masculinity that restricts intimate connection
with life threatens all living creatures. When a man ignores
his desire for connection, purpose, and meaning, it can make
him physically sick or emotionally weak because his soul is
running on empty. The soul of a man aches for meaning and
to live a life that makes a positive difference to himself and
others.

Liberating masculinity, however, opens men up and encourages intimate connections in all relationships. Expanding
manhood toward a fuller expression of our humanity leads to
great rewards. The antidote to our loneliness and isolation is
found in both developing a compassionate mindset and moving toward meaningful and intimate connections with others
and with our natural environment.

But men seem to find it difficult to connect with other men
unless there is some task or agenda to fulfill. A man calling or
inviting another man to lunch "just to talk" is not common.
Men tend to connect with other men in the process of some
activity like sports, working on a car, professional meetings,
or social events involving couples. Once a man is married and
becomes involved with family, his friendships with other men
are often treated as unimportant, or something to fit into a
schedule and between chores.

Connection Complications

There are a number of reasons why men avoid close connection with other men. The first, and perhaps most powerful reason, is the pervasive and ill-fated presence of homophobia, which is defined as fear of, aversion to, or discrimination against homosexuality or homosexuals. Sometimes, homophobia describes the fear of feeling or expressing love toward men. Homophobic men often spread their fear and prejudice toward people with any variation of sexual expression, including lesbian, bisexual, or transgender individuals. Homophobic men seem to follow a rule that goes something like, "If you aren't like me, I will fear and be hostile toward you." These beliefs and reactions to diverse sexual expressions are hallmarks of confined masculinity. As a consequence, homophobic men often overgeneralize and avoid identifying feelings or talking about deeper emotions with other men. In fact, Ed Adams has met men who have never expressed intimate feelings to any other man in their entire life.

And yet, in early America, our culture prized lasting and intimate friendships between men. As historian Richard Godbeer states, "Early Americans assumed that the structure and well-being of society were determined by the dynamics and tone of personal relationships, especially those between family members and also between close friends who saw themselves as elective kinfolk." There exist many love letters, letters of intimate appreciations and deep emotional expression between men that suggest this was a natural way to feel toward other men in the era of our founding fathers. Being closely connected with other men held no stigma. Godbeer writes, "Most Anglo-Americans living in the colonial and revolutionary periods treated emotional ties between male friends as quite distinct from sexual desire."[6] Today, homophobia prevents men from becoming close to one another.

The important factor is this: "masculine" behavior is subject to change through social evolution. We all lose when male-to-male relationships are feared and neglected. Just like compassion, connection does not deserve to be caked with judgment and avoidance.

No man, straight or gay, has connection and community figured out perfectly. Loneliness can creep into the lives of any gay man and older gay men in particular. Many older gay men lost lovers and friends during the worst of the AIDS crisis decades ago. And as gay men hit forty and beyond, they struggle to maintain close bonds with others, says Dusty Araujo, a community organizer based in San Francisco. Araujo says aging gay men no longer fit easily into a social scene of bars and clubs, nor are they very comfortable with social media dating tools geared to the gay population. "You become invisible," Araujo says. "Where does the fifty-year-old gay man go to meet someone?"

But Araujo and others are working on the problem. He is program coordinator of the Elizabeth Taylor 50-Plus Network, an initiative of San Francisco AIDS Foundation designed to promote wellness, friendships, and community service among gay, bisexual, and transgender men fifty years and older. One of the 50-Plus Network's activities is a gathering every Saturday morning at Maxfield's House of Caffeine, a café on the edge of San Francisco's Castro District—one of the major hubs of gay culture worldwide. Roughly twenty to twenty-five men regularly attend the Maxfield's events. They greet each other with hugs, kisses, smiles, and laughs.

It is a very diverse set of men. Some of them own homes, while some are homeless. Some have graduate degrees, while others have little education. "What brings us together is that we are over fifty and we survived the HIV epidemic," Araujo says. That common ground, and the ability for men to share their experiences in a safe place, keeps them returning to the group.

"We bring people back from isolation into community," he says.[7]

To Connect or Not to Connect

Araujo himself is a striking example of how reaching out to others leads to a richer life. The seventy-one-year-old was born in Panama. He says he was very self-centered until he and his former partner adopted two children thirty years ago. The responsibility to care for his son and daughter transformed his perspective. It led him to take a series of jobs in nonprofit and activist groups, including his current role at San Francisco AIDS Foundation. On his backpack is a pin with the word ME supported by the word WE.

"Having a child made me focus outside of me," Araujo says. "It made me realize you can't base your life on you alone. You have to focus on the other direction."[8]

Still, some men take pride in isolation. This occurs when isolation is seen as being self-sufficient, independent, and manly. These men explain their preference for isolation and claim that being alone is easier, less demanding, and free of obligations. Certain men who desire friendships don't know how to go about making friends. One man told Ed Adams that you "can't go online and find a best friend." And since making male friends is difficult, some men avoid connecting with others because it generates anxiety.

Think of it this way. Movement toward liberating masculinity requires holding a variety of positive and negative emotions while taking constructive action. It can be like a tiny clown car with a dozen clowns inside. In order to increase your social network and develop friendships, you must take anxieties, doubts, excitement, fear of rejection, discomfort, unpredictability, and social awkwardness along with you. In short, you are more likely to build social connections when you bring these feelings along for the ride—rather than waiting for them to go away before taking action. Every man attending his first Men Mentoring Men (M3) meeting comes with all or many of these feelings. The victory is in showing up. Then, after a meeting or two, most of these anxieties fade.

Men Loving Men

Ed Adams recalls a particular men's meeting that became a watershed moment in the thirty-year history of M3. Over a three-year period, a group of fifteen to twenty men were meeting together every other week. Most of the participants felt emotionally safe to disclose intimate, or A-level, matters with the other men. Then, one member described how he'd followed the group's advice and how the suggestion had helped resolve a particularly difficult issue in his life. He said,

"I want you all to know how much you guys mean to me and how helpful you have been. I want to thank you and I lo… lo…you. I mean I…I—" Then another man said, "love you?" Everyone smiled. The first man said, "Yes, I love you." The men knew this was not a romantic love but a "philia" love—a brotherly love comprised of appreciation, gratitude, compassion, and connection. This man didn't know it at that time, but he'd activated the very opposite of homophobia, while shifting everyone involved deeper into liberating masculinity.

Within M3 today, the fear of men loving each other has become desexualized, and it's not uncommon for love to be expressed among the men. The gay and trans men who participate in M3 find comfort and safety in the company of men, straight or gay, willing to be loving friends. The men of M3 prove that it's not necessary to fear love and sexuality. In fact, connections with others are good for your health and overall well-being, as well as for society. Our forefathers knew this; they were on to something important and soulful.

It would be difficult to find research that showed social connection to be detrimental to your health. That's because our need for connection is built into our DNA. The fear of connecting is learned. In today's world, we seem to be more prone to isolation despite the ubiquity of social media. As mentioned before, the antidote to loneliness and isolation is not only in the recognition of it, but in behaviors that create and deepen relationships. Change requires action. Get into the clown car of life with all of your doubts and fears; turn on the ignition and go make connections. Make intimacy happen.

Connections at Work

This advice includes making connection and intimacy happen at work. If you do, you're liable to zip ahead and manage bumps in the road that are coming faster and faster. But if you don't connect deeply with others, you may find yourself getting left behind. You may find yourself booted off the bus of your current employer—and have a hard time getting aboard another.

Put simply, connection skills are critical business skills in the economy that's emerging. We'll say more about this in the next chapter. But the main message is that a faster pace of change, increased demographic diversity, and technological advances all are creating workplaces that penalize men who are rigid, cold, and isolated. Men aiming to succeed at work need to move away from that confined masculinity approach to a liberating masculinity mode of flexibility, warmth, and collaboration. This isn't to say that men should discard independent work, dispassionate analysis, and principled stands. But those elements have to be harmonized with the ability to be more emotionally open and more deeply connected.

Connection with Life

Leo Buscaglia, an educator and author of many inspirational books, was considered a "cheerleader for life." Dr. Buscaglia proclaimed that if you're bored, you're boring. Ed Adams heard those words during a stressful time in his life, so he found them difficult to accept. Truthfully, he was very bored with himself. He had been laser-focused for months completing his dissertation. He believed it was the only important thing in life. Once it was finished, Ed's life felt empty and aimless. He resented the suggestion that he had anything to do with this pervasive, uncomfortable feeling. Eventually, despite his resistance, Ed took note of Buscaglia's wisdom and finally admitted that he was boring himself to death. "My soul was withering on the vine," Ed recalls.

Ed decided to de-bore himself. He began this journey with curiosity and challenging questions. What do I really care about? What activities engage my imagination? What am I afraid of? Who do I find interesting and why? And what does my boredom want from me?

He began to notice that every answer to these questions included one major ingredient: connection. Expanding life involves connecting more deeply and broadly with others, because infinite experiences and possibilities come from those ties.

Liberating masculinity occurs when we deepen our creative connections to others and to everything around us. One way to deepen our connection to life is to apply the following five steps in your relationships, career, and life interests. And while you will likely recognize a sexual parallel to these steps, the point is simply to generate a more connected, intimate, and creative life.

GET TURNED ON: Be attracted to life as it is, not how you wish it to be. Know that you are enough of a man to live, love, and prosper.

BECOME ERECT: Be ready to move into the possibilities of life and allow the places and things you enjoy to focus your attention.

PENETRATE: Move deeply into your relationships, interests, skills, and life choices. Become a subject matter expert.

FERTILIZE: Give new energy to your relationships and interests.

NURTURE: Protect and strengthen what you created and help it grow.

These five steps are interrelated. For example, if you are not turned on to life, then the other four steps will shut down. If you are turned on and excited but you don't take risks or move deeply into your ideas, projects, relationships, and skills, there will be nothing to show for your prior efforts. And if you do the first four steps but don't provide, protect, strengthen, and nurture what you created, it will likely fall apart.

We began this chapter with the story about Roy's experience of loneliness and isolation. Roy was a therapeutic challenge for Ed because he believed his fate was to be forever alone, his destiny sealed. Because of these beliefs, he resisted making changes. Fortunately, he went on a dating site and had lunch with a woman who saw the acorn inside Roy's heart. They began to date and eventually moved in together.

Roy developed new acquaintances, joined M3, and became interested in photography. And though Roy is an introvert, he is no longer isolated and alone. After so many sessions of Ed seeing Roy lonely and wistful, the fact that Ed now sees him relating, laughing and smiling is priceless.

THINGS TO PONDER AND DO

CURIOSITY: Is there someone you'd like to get to know better? Connect with that person and do something together.

COURAGE: Connection requires courage. Make a list of all that you fear or worry about, and then imagine all of them piling into your emotional "clown car." Then take action to connect.

COMPASSION: Be gentle with yourself and self-compassionate regarding your connections with other men. Our culture makes it difficult and challenging to develop male friendships. Instead of beating yourself up, appreciate the steps you take.

CONNECTION: Connections grow down. This means that you can deepen the roots of existing relationships if you are more kind, emotionally generous, and involved. Try to go beyond your typical comfort level with someone you are already connected to. Let go of any homophobia you may have and express tender feelings you may have toward another man.

COMMITMENT: Find a man or group of men with whom you can relearn how to be playful, trusting, and self-disclosing. Promise yourself that male companionship will not be neglected or marginalized.

Ways and Means

6 Reinventing Masculinity at Work

ED FRAUENHEIM

Confined masculinity isn't working anymore at work. Just ask Travis Marsh.

Travis grew up with many of the beliefs and behaviors that define a traditional man. He was ambitious, he was a high achiever, he was self-assured. These traits aren't inherently toxic. But they came packaged with self-centeredness and indifference to peers' overall well-being. This confined masculinity combination proved to be poisonous as Travis pursued a career in business.

After graduating from the University of Florida in 2004 with a degree in mechanical engineering, Travis took a job at an electronics company, National Instruments in Austin, Texas. He did well initially, advancing from a support role to a sales engineer job to a sales manager position in four short years. That last promotion put him in charge of an eight-person team in his late twenties. And when he took the role, he managed people using a method that roughly fit into his version of masculinity: an autocratic, controlling, callous style.

Those weren't the terms Travis used. Instead, he borrowed

a widely used euphemism for constantly checking in on what those under him were doing. "I called it 'visibility,'" Travis says. "But it was really micromanagement."

He had no concept of work–life balance and expected his team to work the same long days he did. And while he said all the right things about supporting his subordinates' progress, their triumphs took a back seat to his own goals of winning sales awards and climbing the corporate ladder.

"I wanted them to succeed," Travis recalls. "But I had a pretty narrow definition of what success looked like—and it was what mattered for me."

With this me-first perspective, goal fixation, and top-down mode of leadership, Travis's upward trajectory hit a hard ceiling. His team was behind on its target and going in the wrong direction. This was the case even though they sold products in a fast-growing niche and several members of his team had such promise that they were selected for a leadership development program.

The Trouble with Travis— and with Confined Masculinity at Work

What was Travis's problem? For one thing, a dictatorial style has long led to dispirited employees and mediocre results. Travis's leadership approach also ran counter to the way the young people on his team wanted to work. Most of them were millennials, a generation raised and schooled to have a say over what they're doing. Millennials also tend to prioritize a meaningful life beyond work, and often are willing to sacrifice promotions in favor of pursuing their personal passions and relationships. By prescribing how his young team should perform their jobs and forcing them to work soul-crushing hours, Travis killed their morale and creativity. As a result, Travis was failing to hit his sales targets and all but pushing his people out the door.

"They were not only disengaged," he recalls, "but actively seeking new jobs elsewhere."

Travis's story is the story of an outdated masculinity. Confined masculinity, with its stoicism, fixed viewpoints, and isolation, no longer serves men individually nor our organizations. The business climate is changing in ways that require a different approach both to being a man and to working together.

While a debate has raged in our popular culture about whether men are getting too soft, a quiet consensus has developed in the organizational world: today, soft skills are success skills. Compassion and connection—along with their cousins cooperation, communication, empathy, and generosity itself— have become critical to individual and team effectiveness. Curiosity, which requires vulnerability, is also vital in an economy that demands constant learning and ever more agility. In other words, what's called for today is a liberating masculinity.

Men are answering that call. Men in many professions, industries, and countries are showing the way forward. So are leading organizations. From professional sports teams to tech firms to construction companies, cutting-edge organizations are moving away from obsolete, demeaning, machine-like management styles. They are cultivating higher-performing,

Good Sportsmanship

A reinvention of masculinity is underway in one of the industries that most rewards outstanding performance: professional sports.

Professional male athletes and coaches are among the pioneers moving to a liberating masculinity. This might seem surprising at first glance. If liberating masculinity is about curbing competition in favor of collaboration, how does that work for teams vying to win championships? It turns out that sports teams are listening to the latest science on organizational success—the same insights that are prodding the business world overall to embrace empathy, decentralized power, and shared purpose. Players, coaches, and owners also are learning from today's sports leaders, who are demonstrating a different kind of masculinity from the male athlete icons of yore.

Look for items below to see how men like Tom Brady, Steve Kerr, and Stephen Curry are illustrating the power—and joy—of compassion and connection.

human-centered, life-giving cultures. In effect, men are working to reinvent masculinity at work—and it's working.

This chapter documents the shift at work underway in the twenty-first century. It explains how a confined masculinity is poorly suited for the emerging landscape, both because it fails to prepare men to prosper today and because it all but prevents them from seeing positive solutions to our collective economic problems. Liberating masculinity, the chapter will show, offers a hopeful way forward at work—for men as individuals, for our organizations and for us as a global society.

Observing and Advancing the World of Work

I've had a front-row seat to the way work has been changing. And I've been working on work myself. For two decades I was a journalist focused on work, business, and technology. I've spent the past six years as a writer and researcher at Great Place to Work, a global advisory firm with workplace-culture expertise. We are best known for conducting the analysis behind the annual *Fortune* 100 Best Companies to Work For list.

At Great Place to Work, I've been able to study the very best organizations on the planet. The results of our anonymous employee survey show that people in these top organizations trust leaders, take pride in their jobs, and feel a sense of camaraderie. Along with several colleagues, I cowrote the 2018 book *A Great Place to Work for All*—which includes my interviews with employees ranging from executives to frontline workers in Brazil, India, and Italy, among other countries.[1]

What's more, in 2018 I cofounded the Teal Team, a group devoted to helping organizations become more democratic, purpose-driven, soulful places. I share more on this group later on.

One of the lessons I've learned from observing and advocating for great workplaces is that work matters to men. By and large, men want to do a good job. And they want their work to be about more than a paycheck. Author Studs Turkel

No "I" in Team

Have you noticed that winning pro sports teams in the past couple of decades have been teams that are especially, well, team-y? To be sure, teamwork and sacrificing individual success for the good of the group have always been important to team sports. But for much of the twentieth century, the focus was on the star players who just happened to be surrounded by subordinate "role" players. Think of icons like Babe Ruth, Joe Montana, and Michael Jordan.

Increasingly, though, leading sports teams are paying attention to the bonds among all their players. They are seeking to cultivate relationships off the court in order to optimize performance on it. And these teams have found that the whole is much greater than the sum of the parts. This is true of the San Francisco Giants in baseball, the New England Patriots in football, and the San Antonio Spurs in basketball.* These championship

* "Lessons from Super Bowl Legends Tom Brady and Bill Belichick on Teamwork and Leadership," Lighthouse Blog, n.d., accessed April 10, 2020, https://getlighthouse.com/blog/tom-brady-and-bill-belichick-leadership-lessons/.

had it right in his book *Working*: work "is about a search…for daily meaning as well as daily bread, for recognition as well as cash, for astonishment rather than torpor; in short, for a sort of life rather than a Monday through Friday sort of dying."[2]

These elegant words fit what I've noticed about men across the globe. I spoke with a hotel concierge in India who took it upon himself to travel hundreds of miles to return identification papers to a guest who'd left them behind.[3] I've written teams have stood out for practices like team dinners, silly dugout rituals to rev each other up, and expressions of brotherly love.

Consider what Patriots quarterback Tom Brady did immediately after winning his record sixth Super Bowl ring. Breaking away from the limelight of the TV cameras, Brady found and hugged people—including an opposing player. "I love you," is what he said, again and again. Putting relationships over personal glory, in a vulnerable way, was in keeping with Brady's humble habit of greeting each new teammate who joined the Patriots. Despite being the most famous player in the league, he always introduced himself, saying: "Hi. I'm Tom Brady."[*]

In effect, Brady and other sports leaders today recognize that a confined masculinity that rules out deep connection and humility is a losing strategy.

[*] Bill Murphy Jr., "Tom Brady Kept Saying 1 Simple Word Over and Over after the Super Bowl (and Taught an Amazing Lesson in Leadership)," *Inc.*, February 4, 2019, https://www.inc.com/bill-murphy-jr/tom-brady-kept-saying-1-simple-word-over-over -after-super-bowl-it-tells-you-everything-you-need-to-know-about-leadership.html.

about security guards in Peru who transformed their profession from a low-status role to one full of honor, integrity, and playfulness—complete with a hip music video. I've spoken with Jeff Green, a U.S. executive who protected the dignity of his employees by firing a manager who treated her team poorly, even though she herself got great results.[4]

"It was one of the toughest conversations I've had," said Green, CEO of advertising technology firm The Trade Desk.

But Green made the hard decision based on a vision of his nine-hundred-employee company as a close-knit family. "We're building something of a home," he told me. "This is where we live. And this is where we want to be for a long time."

Confined Masculinity at Work

Despite heartwarming anecdotes like these, the history of the work world has been disheartening in many ways. It is rife with exploitation, wasted human potential, and environmental destruction. The grim story has much to do with a confined version of manhood.

After all, our organizations for centuries have largely reflected a traditional, confined masculinity. Companies have featured strict hierarchical structures defined by a command-and-control approach to leadership. Those at the top—usually men—have established competitive cultures that prize efficiency. Emotions are all but forbidden and employees often vie against each other for ever-higher positions of authority. Overall, the goals of capitalist corporations have matched those of confined men: maximum profits and power—typically defined as market share—with minimal concern about people or planet.

To be fair, such organizations have generated great wealth and created products and technology that have enhanced human well-being. They have built soaring cathedrals, helped send men to the moon, and created miniscule computer chips that now power ever-more-advanced artificial intelligence.

But all the progress in creating miraculous machines has come at a cost. We have treated workplaces themselves as machines with little room for our humanity. For more than two centuries, people have decried the dehumanizing, degrading quality of industrial capitalist companies. The eighties rock group The Police nailed it in their song "Synchronicity II," which lamented the life of a suburban company man: "Every single meeting with his so-called superior is a humiliating kick in the crotch."[5]

Such problems have persisted as the economy has shifted to the Information Age. Only about one-third of American workers are engaged on the job, a number that drops to about 15 percent when you look at employees worldwide.[6] In effect, the bulk of organizations in the United States and across the globe are deadening places for the people who work there.[7]

A Masculinity That Makes Less Cents

Thankfully, the days of "military general" CEOs, sterile environments, and isolated and irresponsible enterprises are drawing to a close. Simply put, confined masculinity makes less and less sense—and cents—in the twenty-first century.

In the Industrial Age, there was some logic to treating the men and women operating factory equipment as mindless cogs, as worker ants. But the opposite imperative exists today. As we enter an era of digital disruption and advanced robots, human qualities such as creativity, passion, and collaborative spirit are increasingly vital, since organizations aim to constantly innovate, adjust to fast-changing market conditions, and provide personalized, memorable experiences to customers.[8]

Traditional organizations are increasingly at risk as the business climate becomes flatter, faster, and more fairness-focused. Organizations find themselves challenged to become more diverse and inclusive, more attuned to the needs of their communities and the environment, more willing to distribute power, and more capable of sensing and responding to emerging signals. Those demands, in turn, put authoritarian chains of command at a disadvantage. Top-down structures are proving to be too slow in a quicker, more complex commercial arena.[9]

In other words, the confined masculinity style of bosses giving *directions* will have to give way to providing overall *direction*. Leaders will need to concentrate on painting the big picture, connecting employees to that purpose, and trusting people to make good decisions and generate good ideas.

As it stands, the average American company operates at just a fraction of its potential to innovate and grow. My colleagues and I at Great Place to Work learned that just two U.S. employees have many opportunities to innovate at work for every six employees who have few to no such opportunities. Great Place to Work also discovered that the organizations racing ahead in terms of inventions and agility—such as computer chip maker Nvidia and grocery chain Wegmans Food Markets—act more like a flock of birds or a school of fish than a rigid pyramid of management layers with a boss at the top.[10] They are moving away, that is, from a business model that resembles confined masculinity.

Confined Men of Steel

Not surprisingly, other companies are following innovation leaders like Nvidia and Wegmans. And this transition is difficult for men bound by traditional man-rules. Many of these men, especially in leadership positions, have tried to be like Superman at work. They've aimed to be strong, confident, virtually invincible, and able to save the day single-handedly. But when men emulate the man of steel, they often act in ways that no longer serve them: with emotional indifference, hyper-competitiveness, aggression, and isolation.[11]

Consider the example of Travis from earlier in this chapter. He was trying to do it all as a young manager. But his brashness and ambition, combined with little regard for the input or work-life balance of his team, made him a horrific supervisor. "I was a world-class asshole," he admits in retrospect.

This was the case despite good intentions. He wanted to be a great leader for his team. But the confined masculinity norms he had absorbed while growing up got in the way. Norms about superiors and subordinates. About those rising up being able send orders down to those on the front lines. About obedience. "I didn't even realize these were the norms that I was internalizing," Travis says. "I espoused caring about an inclusive environment. I just didn't know how to do that and also deliver results."

What Travis didn't understand at the time is that the best results today are coming not from heroic leaders but from effective teams. Work today is becoming a team sport. The most innovative discoveries and most nimble operations require breaking down silos in organizations and bringing together people with diverse perspectives and talents. This means collaboration and persuasion are more productive than solo displays of dominance.

The key to successful teams at one of the most successful companies in the twenty-first century—Google—turns out to be "psychological safety."[12] Caring, rather than scaring, produces the best results today.[13]

From Confined to Expanding at Work

Consider the profile of success in the workplace that's emerging. It's long been true that emotional intelligence and self-awareness are more important to leaders as they assume higher-ranking posts.[14] But amid the growing importance of soft skills, more and more companies are seeking vulnerability, empathy, and listening skills in leaders and front-line employees alike.

Organizations also are looking for generous spirits. Scholar Adam Grant has found that the best performers today tend to be people who give more than they take. The most successful "givers" outperform not only "takers" but also "matchers," those who try to mirror the generosity of others. "Givers succeed in a way that creates a ripple effect," Grant writes, "enhancing the success of people around them."[15]

Another emerging requirement is sensitivity around working with people of different backgrounds—and awareness of one's own privileges and biases. Even though men and women have been expected to treat each other fairly and with respect for decades, those expectations have intensified. True

All for One and One for All

Coauthor Ed Adams's alma mater is Xavier University in Cincinnati, Ohio. Their school mascot is a musketeer and the school motto is "All for One and One for All." In the business world that's emerging, the Three Musketeers' slogan is proving to be a recipe for success.

My colleagues and I at Great Place to Work found that organizations that create the most consistently positive experience for all their employees—no matter who they are or what they do for the company—race ahead of the competition. Those organizations, called Great Workplaces to Work for All, enjoy more than three times the revenue growth of less-inclusive peers.*

*See Michael C. Bush and the Great Place to Work Research Team, *A Great Place to Work for All: Better for Business, Better for People, Better for the World* (Oakland, CA: Berrett-Koehler Publishers, 2018), https://www.greatplacetowork.com/book.

workplace equity increasingly isn't seen as just the right thing to do, but as providing a boost to business results thanks to better ideas and decision-making.

The new approach to success at work is captured by the concept of the "for all" leader. My colleagues and I at Great Place to Work came up with this term in the course of studying 10,000 managers and 75,000 employees. We discovered that the most effective, inclusive leaders—whom we dubbed "For All Leaders"—had traits such as humility, the ability to build bonds of trust with and among team members, and a focus on a bigger purpose rather than immediate results.[16]

Humble, Happy Warriors

Mutual affection, muted egos, and shared purpose define the highly successful Golden State Warriors basketball team. The team's run of championships began under coach Steve Kerr. Kerr, who played under San Antonio Spurs coach Gregg Popovich, created a set of team values that included compassion along with competition, joy, and mindfulness. With these guiding principles, the Warriors took teamwork to another level.

To be sure, the team had superstar scorers in Stephen ("Steph") Curry and Kevin Durant. But they also stood out for having the most assists in the league—a sign of the cooperative, unselfish play that leads to easy baskets. They also played team defense with such communication and awareness of each other that one observer described them this way: "They are tied together. Think of the Warriors on defense as five Swiss mountain climbers, moving in calculated rhythm."*

This level of collaboration requires tame egos. In fact, Steph

*Scott Ostler, "Warriors United in the Poetry of Defense," *San Francisco Chronicle*, April 13, 2017, https://www.sfchronicle.com/sports/ostler/article/Warriors-united-in-the -poetry-of-defense-11071364.php.

This is a far cry from the kind of combativeness, bravado, and stoicism that confined masculinity calls for.

Confined men are often stiff, cold, and isolated in a work world now calling for flexibility, warmth, and connection. More and more, men trying to follow the rules of confined masculinity in the emerging workplace are finding they don't fit in. Many are limping along. Some are being let go.

Curry put his pride aside when the team acquired Durant—a move that enabled the team to win consecutive championships. "If you win MVP or I win MVP, it doesn't matter," Curry told Durant in a text. "We're trying to win championships. And if you do win, I'll be in the front row clapping for you at the press conference."*

Superstars and teams of old were more driven by chips on shoulders, by ego and anger. Michael Jordon wore a scowl just like the one on the Chicago Bulls logo. But more and more, the leading teams of today are about smiles and laughter. They are about the giddy shoulder shimmies of Steph Curry.

In fact, the pleasure of connection goes hand in hand with positive results in sports today. The liberation, the release of playing loose with close-knit teammates, leads to success. As one sports writer said about the Warriors: "Joy is a weapon, an essential aspect of winning. Their fun is your demise."**

*Arlos Sara, "Stephen Curry's Lack of Ego Played a Big Part in Recruiting Kevin Durant," *ClutchPoints*, September 14, 2016, https://clutchpoints.com/stephen-currys-lack-ego-played-big-part-recruiting-kevin-durant/.
**Ethan Strauss, "To the 15-0 Warriors, Joy Is a Weapon," *ESPN*, November 22, 2015, https://www.espn.com/blog/golden-state-warriors/post/_/id/925/to-the-15-0-warriors-joy-is-a-weapon.

A Confusing, Frustrating Economy for Confined Men

Confined men not only are struggling in today's organizations, they are experiencing our wider economy as confusing and frustrating as well. The trends of globalization, automation, and decreasing unionization have led to increasing job insecurity, personal financial instability, and overall economic inequality. Men with less formal education especially have felt the brunt of these big forces. Manufacturing jobs have been moved overseas or eliminated by robots. Entire communities in developed countries like the United States and the United Kingdom have felt their economic foundation shaken, and seen social problems like opioid addiction rise.

Add to this something that must feel like an insult on top of injury to men constrained by traditional views of "men's work." Many of the new jobs replacing factory jobs and other blue-collar positions are in "helping" professions historically associated with women. Job growth is in fields like nursing, education, customer service, and hospitality.[17]

A winner-take-all economy, the prospect of mass unemployment thanks to automation, shattered individual dreams, and frayed social fabrics are all real problems. Reforms are needed. These include stronger safety nets, more-progressive tax schemes, fairer international trade rules, and labor protections for people forced into the "gig" economy—that is, into insecure, contract jobs like Uber driving.

But confined masculinity inhibits a clear view of our global socio-economic system. Instead, an isolated perspective, a penchant for competing rather than cooperating, and a mindset of scarcity is pushing many men deeper into a defensive crouch. A cynical, dangerous crouch. Many men are adopting an us-versus-them mindset and demonizing others, including rival political parties, immigrants, and foreign nations. Confined men also balk at the need to build an economy that addresses the climate crisis. Indeed, many deny the human-generated impact on the environment and reject efforts to prevent a planetary catastrophe.[18]

Liberating Masculinity Gets to Work

It's a different, more hopeful story with liberating masculinity. Men with this version of manhood are better able to understand today's growing economic complexity. They are inclined to see the interconnections of people, companies, nations, and the earth itself. With this systems perspective, they are more equipped to propose solutions that account for our interdependence, and that leave no one behind.

While working on the larger, societal level to fix problems, liberating men also are finding success in the workplace today. Men like Paul.

Paul is a longtime member of M3. When he first joined more than twenty years ago, Paul was working as an accountant, following a typical male path to career success. But he hated the job. His calling had always been to be a nurse, and the men of M3 encouraged him to be true to himself. So, a few years into his participation in M3, Paul made the switch to nursing.

And he has thrived. Not only does Paul love his work in a New Jersey hospital, but he has advanced professionally. While continuing to provide nursing care directly to patients, Paul also took on managerial responsibilities. One of his initiatives was to encourage EMT professionals to demonstrate more compassion in the hospital. He had noticed EMTs in the ER—around patients—using dark humor and acting callously, behavior Paul chalked up to self-protection amid much suffering and sadness. He says his efforts to promote greater kindness at work, and ultimately more effective healing, stem from how he has matured as a man.

"I wouldn't have pushed for this change if I hadn't experienced the benefit of trying to become more compassionate myself," Paul says. "Most of us, men and women, can treat one another better. And it makes a difference for patients."

Paul isn't alone in bringing a liberating, expanding masculinity to work—and finding greater happiness as a result.

Some of these other men fly in the face of stereotypes that say only college-educated men can escape the plight of confined masculinity. Take Greg, a sensitive and competent owner of a construction company who moved into his family's business after completing high school. Greg is another M3 member who has infused his work life with a bigger way of being a man. He has changed as a boss over the years. Having regular conversations with other men about hopes and fears, joy and sadness prompted him to view his thirty-five employees—who are mostly men—in a different light, and to manage with a lighter touch. "I definitely went from being 'balls to the wall' to actually thinking about the guys," he says. "You step back from being the owner or the boss to thinking, 'Well, there's a little kid that wants their dad to show up to tee-ball or their band concert.'"

Liberating Masculinity, at Firms Small and Large

It's not only at small businesses where men are leading in new ways. You can find liberating masculinity taking root at the world's largest organizations.

Consider Chuck Robbins. Robbins is the CEO of Cisco Systems, the data networking and communications technology company that employs 74,000 people across the globe.

Not long after he took the reins of Cisco in 2015, Robbins had a vivid and disturbing dream. In it, Robbins visited a homeless encampment, where he saw the faces of his pastor and his father. The dream inspired him to take action on the homelessness that plagues San Jose, the Silicon Valley city that Cisco calls home.

"The next day, I called the mayor," Robbins told me. "I said, 'I want to get involved in solving this problem.'"[19] What happened next was a surge of social responsibility at Cisco. For starters, the company made a $50 million, five-year donation to Destination: Home, a nonprofit group devoted to ending homelessness in the San Jose region. And Robbins's commitment to giving back proved contagious. Or, to hear him say it, his visibility on homelessness simply prompted Cisco employees around the world to share with others what they were already doing to serve their communities—as well as to increase their efforts.

"There's this immense desire to give back," Robbins says. "We just made it okay. People have embraced it. It's blown me away."

Note that the philanthropy hasn't distracted Robbins from traditional business goals. Under his leadership, Cisco launched a new subscription networking gear service—the fastest growing product in the company's history. On the strength of the new service, Cisco stock rose to its highest point in twenty years.

Robbins says the business boost was fueled by doing the right thing, because employees everywhere are fired up to work at a company they're proud of. Indeed, Cisco became Great Place to Work's #1 World's Best Workplace under

Robbins's leadership. And in the long run, Robbins argues, if powerful organizations like Cisco don't take the lead on social problems, our global future will look more like a nightmare than a dream.

"We have to cultivate healthy communities," he says. "Or it's not going to work for anybody."

Robbins isn't the only captain of industry to define social responsibility as a business priority. He's a member of Business Roundtable, a group of CEOs who in 2019 declared "a fundamental commitment to all of our stakeholders"—not just shareholders.[20]

From the Man of Steel to Men of Teal

In the growing conversation about elevating the way we work—a discussion in which people of both sexes and all gender identities are weighing in—it is encouraging that men are playing constructive roles. Men, in effect, are rethinking workplaces that often benefited them to the detriment of others. For example, men are actively promoting the "Agile" approach to work, which replaces top-down agendas with collaborative teamwork. Men are also central to the Conscious Capitalism community, a network of business leaders who are "dedicated to elevating humanity through business."[21]

Men also are key players in the "teal" movement to transform our workplaces into soulful, life-giving places. As author Frederic Laloux writes in *Reinventing Organizations*, a teal mindset involves a "deep yearning for wholeness—bringing together the ego and the deeper parts of the self; integrating mind, body, and soul; cultivating both the feminine and masculine parts within; being whole in relation to others; and repairing our broken relationship with life and nature."[22]

Laloux was building on various scholars' work exploring the stages of human development. Within that scholarship, teal is part of a color scheme describing levels of human consciousness and refers to an awareness that all life is interdependent. A teal consciousness also aims to replace our deep-seated fears with a mindset of trust—both trust in each other and trust in how life unfolds. Organizations embracing teal principles put purpose ahead of profits, enable employees to manage themselves, and honor the holistic needs of people and the planet.[23]

Teal companies have shown great success in conventional terms like revenue growth and market share. They also are attracting people who want out of the rat race and the way it can reduce us to our worst instincts.

The movement toward teal organizations, in other words, overlaps closely with what liberating masculinity looks like at work. You could say we need to stop trying to be the *man of steel* and start becoming *men of teal.*[24]

A Tealy Travis

Perhaps surprisingly, one man who made this change is Travis. His journey out of a confined masculinity began at a low point, when his sales team was dysfunctional and at risk of missing its goals. Travis did some soul-searching, read more about management, and decided to experiment with a radically different approach.

Instead of telling his team what to do and how to do it, Travis decided to listen. He shared the overall challenge they faced—the fact that they were 20 percent below their six-month sales target. And he asked for their ideas. The main choice boiled down to concentrating on a small portion of customers that generated the bulk of the division's sales, or continuing to knock on a wide variety of doors—even though most of the other clients provided much lower revenue on each sale.

Travis's own analysis suggested doubling down on the big-ticket customers. But his team as a group preferred the other strategy. Despite deep doubts, Travis gave their vision the green light. And then he watched the green come rushing in.

"Holy hell, did they make it work," he recalls. The team made up the deficit, raking in about $10 million in a half-year period. Travis chalked up the success to a fire in the bellies of his colleagues, who finally had a say in the direction of their unit. "The wrong strategy with energized people becomes the right strategy," Travis says. "It was the hustle that made it happen."

The power he'd unleashed with a different kind of leadership prompted him to move toward a different kind of masculinity at work. He discovered Laloux's book, and found it so inspiring that he in turn cowrote a book, *Reinventing Scale-Ups,* about how start-up company founders can embrace teal principles as they grow their business.[25]

Later, Travis became a business coach, and recently he joined a group I cofounded called the Teal Team. We are a group of business consultants and researchers, about ten men and women, who support each other's personal and professional growth, study teal ideas, and give workshops on how organizations can evolve to match today's complex needs.[26]

Travis's story captures how men today are reinventing masculinity at work. It's still early days in this transformation away from confined ways of behaving, leading, and organizing our workplaces and economy. But men embracing a liberating masculinity are already making a positive difference. They are moving us toward a way for work to work for us all.

THINGS TO PONDER AND DO

CURIOSITY: What masculine style do you tend to bring to work? Can you think of a time you acted like a confined man? What about a time you embraced liberating masculinity?

COURAGE: How can you be more vulnerable at work? If you are a leader, can you ask a member of your team for help, or give them more discretion in their job? If you aren't a leader, can you share a concern or a joy with a coworker?

COMPASSION: Can you be more aware of the hurt, disappointments, or troubles others are experiencing at work? If a colleague is hurting in some way, offer your support and care—even just in the form of listening.

CONNECTION: Who is someone at work you would like to know better? Reach out and deepen your personal relationship with them. Don't let potential prejudices or barriers—like differences in rank—get in the way.

COMMITMENT: Can you pledge to show up more as a liberating man at work tomorrow? Intentionally practice becoming more flexible, warm, and connected.

Soul in Motion

7 Honoring the Soul of Men

EDWARD M. ADAMS

Throughout our discussion of men and masculinities, we often refer to the idea of soul. Our concept of soul is nonreligious. It often walks the edge between visible and invisible realities. It's a nebulous and multilayered concept that begs to be defined and explained. Yet, this creates a conundrum. Once we attempt to define soul, it leaves the world of imagination and is relocated in the domain of cognition. Soul then becomes an object rather than an experience.

Soul is an unseen reality revealed through the full range of human experiences such as awe, wonder, suffering, and confusion. It attends to what "lies beneath the surface" of our experiences.[1] Soul exists when we do our most rational thinking, as well as when we entertain the dark, secret meanderings of our complex and sometimes-twisted minds.

Soul thrives inside the mysteries of life. It wants to wonder and dive into feelings and experiences rather than understand and catalog them. Like night dreams, soul evokes images without constraints. In a dream we can fly or explore phenomena without attention to any particular time or place. We may become sexually aroused, scared out of our wits, or inspired in unexplained ways. Upon awakening, where do these images and experiences go? They are transformed into foggy, elusive impressions that leave only the telltale footprints of the presence of soul.

When a man lovingly watches his son or daughter in a school play or soccer game, something deep inside his soul is fed. When a man tends to his dying parent, his soul is on full alert. When a man admits deep affection for another man or woman, his soul dances. Yet, paradoxically, soul is also revealed when a man acts out of lust, jealousy, or rage. James Hillman, a "father" of archetypal psychology, championed the need for psychology to return to the needs of soul. Hillman maintained that the soul is ignored when we become simplistic, materialistic, and literal. He urged us to listen to soul and be respectful of what soul reveals to us about the depth and complexity of the human experience. A key concept of archetypal psychology is to "stay in the image"—that is, stay in and listen to imagination. "The gift of an image is that it provides a place to watch your soul."[2]

Soul is always present within us and around us. When a man holds a vision of masculinities without antiquated constraints, he is living a soulful manhood. Media talk of "toxic masculinity" and the "right way to be a man" diminishes the soul of masculinity. Defining "appropriate" masculine gender roles dishonors the soul of men. Masculinity remains in crisis because the soul of manhood suffers from inattention, neglect, and disrespect. The journey from confined masculinity to liberating masculinity returns possibilities into soul. A reinvented masculinity releases the soul of men from the restriction and tyranny of literalism back into the world of the archetypal. It places soul within the myth, mystery, and magic of life.

In therapy, men and women often complain of anxiety, fear, avoidance, depression, anger, violence, loneliness, and self-absorption. Popular psychology and self-help gurus offer ways to fix these complaints. Yet it is a delusion to believe we can live a life of unabated peace and comfort. This misconception often separates a man from his own soul and is likely to even worsen his symptoms. That's because suffering is a part of life; life brings suffering along for the ride. And during those tough times the depth of our humanity is exposed. We must listen with an open heart to all of its convoluted revelations. What we hear may include our soul telling us that compassion and self-compassion are the means to soothe and cope with the suffering in our life, and that a higher purpose and an engaged connection with the world as it is can enliven our joys.

When we are fortunate enough to experience periods of delight and tranquility, consider it an influence of the soul—but know that that's not the only place where the soul lives. Soul lives in the muck of life as well as in the delight. It's as comfortable in the presence of awe and wonder as it is in fear and horror. Soul is present as life reveals itself in every breathing moment.

The word "psychology" originated from the Greek word "*psyche*"; "psychology" literally means "study of the soul." Since every man develops a "personal psychology" or "philosophy" of life, every man possesses his own personal soul or inner truths. And so, every man has the responsibility to nurture his soul with trust, wonder, and wisdom. This personal soul experience is intimately connected to the "anima mundi," or soul of the world. That is why our actions or inactions ripple through all of life.

Liberating masculinity honors the soul of men. It welcomes curiosity, diversity, and ambiguity. Liberating masculinity prefers creativity and abhors rigid dogma. It flourishes by being wide open to life and celebrates improvisation. And as a man's notions of masculinity mature, so does his soul. An expanding man understands the absurdities of life, while also holding the intention to fully embrace it. He is able to venture vertically into the depths of his life, and sink into questions that may cause confusion as well as enlightenment. For example, a man may question the value of his daily job. He may become aware of his longing for intimacy and love, or he may yearn for novelty and adventure. He rejects simplistic dichotomous thinking like good/bad, right/wrong, worthy/unworthy, and heaven/hell. He appreciates the twists and turns of life, its complexity and all its shades of gray.

A soulful man understands the value of generosity and love. His self-awareness and intentions link him to his family, friends, community, country, humanity in general, and the environment. He appreciates that his life is a mystery, and that his life matters—his intention matters, and his actions have consequences. His soul grows deep down into the roots of existence with every predictable and unpredictable life experience. A soulful man looks into his shadow self with respect for the power it holds. Then, his response to this power shapes his core values and constructs his essential character.

In these ways, a soulful, liberating man is a man with greater awareness and more expansive possibilities. He becomes increasingly conscious of the interconnectedness of all of life and of the way unseen realities are unfolding in the universe and within himself. This elevated awareness, sometimes called an integral consciousness, is critical today.[3] In our increasingly complex, interdependent world, men need a more mature, soul-friendly mindset—not just in order to flourish as individuals, but also for our species and planet to thrive.

In liberating masculinity, a man comes to see that soul exists in everything. This includes both the animate and inanimate world, because everything participates in our imagination. Picture visiting the Grand Canyon. At first sight, you may experience the profound, and be filled with a sense of awe at the majesty of nature. In that moment, the presence of the sacred is revealed. It humbles us as much as it inspires. We glimpse the eternal contained in the slow forces of nature. The meaning of clock time becomes irrelevant when witnessing the enduring magnificence of nature.

Why is the soul of men important? What relevance and impact does soul have upon the current state of manhood? How is the soul of men honored?

These are vital and legitimate questions. We can't think of a way to reimagine masculinity without pleading that we all pay attention to the soul of masculinity. Without attention to the soul and how it expresses itself, we merely go through the motions of life as though pursuing a multitude of false gods. For example, overly strict interpretations of the male protector and provider roles leave no room for soul to expand. Even the most successful provider can feel empty and devoid of purpose. Since soul is involved in the full spectrum of life, a weakened soul will appear as empty feelings, and will urge isolation from others. Inattention to soul leads to feeling depressed, uninspired, and bored. Imagine eating a superb meal with no taste buds to inform you of the pleasures that could be experienced with each bite.

Unfortunately, any void within our soul is vulnerable to seductive ways to fill the empty feelings. A neglected soul can be attracted to hate, misogyny, prejudice, violence, and social division. A wounded or abandoned soul may try to find solace by overworking, or by spending endless hours devoted to soul-numbing, mindless distractions like computer games or shallow entertainment. Men who overindulge in pornography, drugs, and alcohol often are pleading for purpose and human connection. Men who live lives centered on making money or gaining status long to be validated, to feel that they matter. The pull toward external things that hold no intrinsic value can be psychologically bewitching—especially in a world that is often alienating, highly complex, and increasingly virtual.

A soulful masculinity grows as men move deeper into liberating masculinity. Men who are self-aware and give full honor to their many archetypal dimensions see the world holistically through three distinct yet integrated lenses.

The PRAGMATIC LENS resides in our bodies and minds. This lens enables a man to see the material realities of life. This visible reality is required to survive, thrive, and get on with the business of living.

The COMPASSIONATE AND CONNECTED LENS lives in the poetry of our hearts. It generates a worldview of interconnectedness and interdependence. This lens notices nonvisible realities that give meaning to our relationships, such as love, generosity, kindness, authenticity, and feelings. You can't purchase these experiences in any store or find them online.

The LENS OF THE SOUL resides in imagination. Our imagination generates our overall worldview. It gives us the liberty to engage life with wisdom or irrationality. Soul wants to learn and experience rather than to judge. The lens of the soul offers a vision of the world where aesthetics matter, because beauty and strong emotion feed the soul. It may be the beauty of a painting, the beauty of your child snuggled safely in your arms. On the darker side, soul is awed by the overpowering forces of nature, or by coming to terms with a life-threatening diagnosis. Joyful and difficult times bring attention to the fact that something deeply important is happening.

The integration of these three lenses represents the soulful change men hunger for in life—to live in all three realms. Men have a genuine desire to be free of restrictions and to see life through each of these lenses. Confined masculinity tends to emphasize the pragmatic lens. It imprisons the lens of imagination with rigid rules and dogmatic beliefs, and rejects the compassion and connection lens as being too "feminine."

In effect, confined masculinity has cast out the feminine aspect of soul and spirit—whereas all healthy human souls harmonize the masculine with the feminine. Scholar Matthew Fox laments the way the "Divine Feminine" has been banished, thanks to patriarchy's rise thousands of years ago: "The male soul has been profoundly wounded by this history—as has the female soul. Today, the stakes for finding a Sacred Marriage of the Divine Feminine and Sacred Masculine have never been higher. Our survival hangs in the balance."[4]

But it's not just the survival of our species—and all life on earth—that's at stake. It's also the quality of life of each individual man and woman. When the soulful lens is ignored, men pursue hollow goals; they pursue the dust of "nothingness." This creates further alienation, and a sickness that no medicine can cure. For example, a patient of mine was diagnosed with a medical heart problem. During one of our therapy sessions, this man said, "Doc, if you can help me heal my soul, my heart will take care of itself."

The crisis within the soul of men injects its harm into relationships, families, communities, politics, popular culture, and our treatment of the earth. At the same time, the impact of men who are conscious of soul provides hope and opportunity for redemption within all spheres of life. Redemptive acts occur at both the micro and macro levels. They can be a simple act of kindness toward one individual or an elaborate corporate philosophy that positively affects millions of people. For example, consider the following:

Every time a man provides food and emotional support for his family, his soul is fed.

Every time a man connects with someone who is lonely, he taps into the soul of compassion.

Every time a man encourages rather than shames another person, he intensifies the beauty of soul.

Every time a man attends his child's school function despite being exhausted, he is creating a soulful memory.

Every time we bury someone we love, the pain of loss reveals the soul's need for connection.

Every time a business chooses to pay higher wages to employees rather than fatten executive bonuses, soul is stirred.

Every time our organizations and institutions increase equality and protect the dignity of all men and women, soul and compassion are evoked.

Every time countries take direct action to protect the environment, the soul of the world is nurtured and honored.

When I am doing therapy with individual men or men in groups, or when Ed Frauenheim is working with organizations, we know we can develop strategies that help relieve emotional symptoms or increase productivity and morale. But too often those interventions will not succeed if the soul of the men or the organization is ignored.

Here is an example. When a married couple comes to their first session, the relationship has typically been in distress for quite some time. This couple may describe how they built a life together, parented children, and found satisfaction in their work. But they feel distant, angry, disappointed, and miserable with each other. The word "divorce" has been used and has certainly been thought about. Given that they have good children, money, and property, what can be wrong?

It doesn't take long to uncover the truth. The soul of the marriage went into hiding. It was nearly abandoned, seldom tended to by either party. The relationship has all the tinsel and trimmings but little depth and substance. Substance is created by tending to the soul of the marriage. Attending to the soul of the marriage is like applying emotional epoxy

Life's Assignment

While fulfilling a school assignment, a young art student created a classically inspired painting that looked and felt like many of the master paintings of the past.

"This is a good painting," he thought.

Later, his teacher critiqued the painting as follows:

"It's not you," she said. "It's who you think you should be. You're trying to be an artist without becoming an artist. Creating authentically can't be rushed, and it can take years to unfold. Perhaps you may never truly achieve it. You must unleash your imagination."

Then she instructed her student to repeat this assignment. "Create from your soul," she advised.

That young artist is now an old man and a widely acclaimed artist. Yet, every morning he looks into the mirror and wonders if the assignment will ever be complete.

—E. M. ADAMS

that binds and strengthens two individual parts into a loving whole. The task of therapy is focused on creating enough emotional security between the couple so the soul that fled from fear, neglect, and abuse feels safe to return and participate fully in the life of the relationship.

We know, and we think you know, that the imagination of manhood requires reinvention. We know that masculinities with soul are truly connected to the world even as men struggle with life's absurdities and contradictions. A soulful masculinity possesses the courage to expand and the commitment to make everyday life more alive for all of us. It's a soul that graces the world with kindness, respect, and equanimity.

Likewise, some institutions and organizations are evolving to possess, protect, and nurture soul. Liberating men—in partnership with women—are rethinking the ways we work so as to move away from machine-like cultures that kill the human spirit. The organizations that are emerging from their efforts are great cause for hope, as we saw in the preceding chapter. By putting purpose first, sharing power, and paying attention to people's holistic needs, these emerging organizations are proving to be more agile, productive, and financially sustainable—even as they elevate the soul.

Reimagining masculinity is a human cause that transcends gender. Unless and until men honor soul, soul will dishonor men. Solutions to our complex social issues will be superficial, and the soul of the world will darken. Tending to the sacredness of soul will usher in a paradigm shift that allows us to see beyond ourselves and move us toward what is urgently needed—a soulful and liberating masculinity.

THINGS TO PONDER AND DO

CURIOSITY: The soul thrives in wonder and inquisitiveness. Can you identify three life experiences that "touched your soul"? What accounts for the depths of those memories?

COURAGE: If you follow the trail of your fantasies, where does it take you? What is being revealed to you that may feel uncomfortable?

COMPASSION: Instead of judgment, can you find compassion for someone who emotionally or physically injured you? What can you learn from this experience?

CONNECTION: Look at the objects around you. Pick one that has deep significance, and write a short poem or story to capture what it means to you and why.

COMMITMENT: Resolve to step out of literalism and stay in wonder. Allow imagination to take you on a magic carpet ride that reveals what you really want, need, and feel.

Hope Ascends

CONCLUSION
It's Time to Reinvent Masculinity

Reinventing masculinity is a humbling and audacious task.

We know that as well as anyone. While it's been an honor to write a book about a better, updated way to be a man, both of us Eds have struggled along the way with masculinity issues ourselves. We shared stories with each other about growing up under the standard man-rules. Sometimes we laughed at ourselves. But sometimes we felt sadness, embarrassment, and shame as we recounted mishandled relationships and opportunities bungled because of self-doubts and fear.

We also had to admit that troubling aspects of traditional manhood still show up in our everyday life. Ed Frauenheim talked about losing his temper repeatedly with his wife and kids—classic cases of confined masculinity covering up fear or failure with anger and aggression. In a similar vein, Ed Adams spoke of overreacting to criticism by reproducing the anger he experienced from an alcoholic father.

After all, we're like millions of men: imperfect, but trying to improve. Trying to break out of a limiting, outdated, and dangerous confined masculinity so as to dive deeper into liberating masculinity.

When we began to outline this book, we discussed what its central message should be. Given the troubled state of the world today, the idea that masculinity needed to be reinvented seemed apparent. But what would be included in the reinvented model? What guidelines would be used for such a bold project? The answers were hidden in plain sight. We needed to integrate compassion and connection into the soul of masculinity. We didn't need to invent new masculine characteristics, exactly. We simply needed to validate elements within our humanity that have long inspired men and women.

Compassion is a gender-free trait. The fourteenth Dalai Lama said, "if you want others to be happy, practice compassion. If you want to be happy, practice compassion."[1] Compassion and its cousin, connection, are values that promote love, healing, and cooperation. According to scholar Matthew Lieberman, social connection "is probably the single easiest way to enhance our well-being."[2]

We also realized men needed encouragement to shed a cramped conception of manhood. We needed to recover a wider range of roles, elevate more ways of moving through the world, and extend our sense of community to encompass all of humanity and life itself.

As we take stock of the collective effect to reshape masculinity, we are both more concerned and more hopeful than ever.

We are concerned that the tyranny of confined masculinity could continue to dominate our culture. Confined masculinity is out of step with our times. It is incapable of comprehending or embracing our increasingly diverse, complex, and interdependent world. It prevents men from living full lives, damages and diminishes their relationships, thwarts their success at work, and impedes them from being responsible citizens. This version of manhood often lionizes anger, violence, prejudice, misogyny, fear, oppression, and misunderstanding. And yet the risks of this masculinity are greater still. Its combativeness, selfishness, intolerance, and myopic vision are taking us to the brink of extinction.

But this isn't the only option available—and herein lies our hope. We have the power to redefine masculinity by living the best of our humanity. We have been hardwired to form attachments to one another, to create bonds, and to maintain deep connections with others beyond our immediate tribe as well as with the earth. Every day, every one of us—men and women—participates in creating, maintaining, and changing our cultural beliefs about manhood. The way we talk to each other, our intimate and extended relationships, our practices at work, our political leadership, our religious principles, and the way we parent our children—all are interwoven in our view of manhood.

While this book is written primarily for men, the changes needed to integrate liberating masculinity into our culture will happen much more rapidly and profoundly with the support of women. Men operating from a confined masculinity have constrained and harmed women over a long period of time and in many horrific ways. Among those ways is how women have been co-opted into the confined fold.

Sometimes, to succeed in a "man's world," women themselves have adopted the beliefs and behaviors of confined masculinity. And some women have encouraged the most aggressive and "me" focused traits in men—while dismissing the men striving to expand their conception of masculinity. In these senses, the reinvention of masculinity is everyone's business.

To be clear, we men are responsible for our own liberation. We can no longer avoid the necessary inner work, or expect women to do that work for us. And we have much to do to right the wrongs our gender has done under the influence of confined masculinity. Still, everybody advances when women join hands with men on the journey toward liberating masculinity.

This notion is expressed eloquently by Dr. Holly Barlow Sweet, the first woman president of Division 51, the division of the American Psychological Association committed to the study of men and masculinities. Sweet writes:

> The once-common belief held by many women that men have all the power and privilege and do not suffer ... shortchanges both men and women. Empathy for men's struggles to be free of restrictive sex role norms helps us all. In a zero-sum game approach to gender, the more attention we pay to men, the less attention we have available to pay to women. In a gender empathy approach, the more attention we pay to men, the more women also benefit.[3]

Will you adopt a "gender empathy approach"? Will you show greater compassion toward people, regardless if they are a man, a woman, or someone who declines to define themselves in either category? Will you seek to connect more deeply with those around you, to recognize your shared humanity?

At its core, this is what it means to move toward a liberating masculinity. It's a journey toward greater kindness and love. All human beings have this path available to them, and we invite you to get moving.

To men in particular, we encourage you to walk down the wide and expanding path of liberating masculinity. It doesn't matter where you start. You may be at the far end of the spectrum, believing that men must be hard-bodied, hard-working, and hard-hearted. You may be in the middle, torn between beliefs you grew up with and the sense that there is more to life as a man. Or you may be far along the road—unshackled by outdated rules and helping others to live more freely as well.

There isn't a finish line, or there isn't a single finish line. Enjoy milestones like deep satisfaction at a daughter's high school graduation, a raise at work resulting from improved cooperation, or the collective thrill of helping to build a new community garden or elect a wise leader. Yes, savor those moments.[4] And keep moving. You can always go deeper and further toward a liberating, expansive masculinity.

And you won't be alone. Already, many men are on the move. Men of all ages, races, creeds, nationalities, and sexual orientations are breaking out of a confined masculinity that limits the full expression of their humanity. They are courageously embarking on an intrepid adventure into their hearts and into the shadowy, uncharted corners of their souls. They are facing down fears and finding they can both enlarge their lives and lift up those around them.

Men are fathering their children as never before, connecting and staying involved in their lives. Men are tearing down the forbidding wall of homophobia to connect with other men with love, honesty, integrity, and vulnerability. Diverse sexual orientations and gender expressions are becoming less feared and more integrated into everyday life. Men are becoming more aware of racial bias, and people of color are seen in more and more positions of influence. Social justice matters to many men who see the need for a more loving, compassionate, and connected world.

Many of our organizations now have leaders who are relinquishing top-down, stoic, selfish playbooks in favor of collaboration, caring, and social responsibility. Important questions are being asked about the holistic needs of people at work and about the impact of corporate decisions on the environment. Men, in partnership with women, are reinventing organizations to become more satisfying, sustainable, and soulful.

Still, there is so much more to do. We live in dangerous times. Times that include suspicion, shaming, hatred, and the willingness to harm others for some perceived slight. Microbes and viruses morphing into pandemics can bring out the darkness in our humanity. We see a rise in hate crimes, antisemitism, racial prejudice, unwarranted incarcerations, inequality, and crimes of selfish greed. Both sides of this human coin, the shadow and the light, exist—but only one of them is capable of moving us out of a self-centered "me" perspective and into a "me and we" perspective. The task is to become conscious of the shadow and bring it to light. This enables us to confront ourselves, in the fullness of our nature. Confined masculinity

Reflections

Every morning and night a man looks into seven mirrors. The first mirror reflects a likeness of his father: his eyes, his chin, and his troubles. The second mirror reveals the face he chooses the world to see. If he gazes long enough at the third mirror, it displays his wounds, fears, and scars. In the fourth mirror, he will see the twinkle of a curious little boy with a passion for life and play. Mirror five reflects a soft and gentle face evoked by intimacy and love. The sixth mirror gives evidence of a hairy, raw beast waiting his turn. The seventh mirror exposes his virtue.

At the beginning and end of each day, the seventh image matters most.

—E. M. ADAMS

is not up to that task—but liberating masculinity is. If we wish to live in greater harmony and spiritual growth with each other, then liberating masculinity is essential.

The soul of masculinity refuses to be ignored or replaced by commercialism and shallow relationships. The soul of masculinity may go into hiding, but it will keep knocking at the door of humankind. It knows how important it is to be inside life rather than just being a spectator. Soul wants us to live within today's realities and contradictions while also moving us toward more evolved ways of living together with all sentient beings. Most importantly, the soul of masculinity wants us to be in awe of the wonder and mystery and possibilities of life. By honoring the soul of masculinity, we can forge a compassionate, connected manhood. One that frees us from obsolete, harmful man-rules and enables us to thrive in our relationships, in our work, and in our communities.

The alarm clock is ringing and it won't stop. It's time for each one of us to wake up and move from a confined manhood to a liberating masculinity filled with the power of compassion and connection.

It's time to reinvent masculinity.

With gratitude,

Edward M. Adams and Ed Frauenheim

NOTES

Foreword

1. Dov Cohen, Joseph Vandello, and Adrian K. Rantilla, "The Sacred and the Social: Cultures of Honor and Violence," in *Shame: Interpersonal Behavior, Psychopathology, and Culture,* eds. Paul Gilbert and Bernice Andrews (Oxford: Oxford University Press, 1998), 261–82.

2. Paul Gilbert, *Living Like Crazy* (York, U.K.: Annwyn House, 2018). See pages 1 and 12.

3. Christopher Ryan, *Civilized to Death: The Price of Progress* (New York: Avid Reader Press/Simon & Schuster, 2019).

4. Robin I. M. Dunbar, "The Social Brain Hypothesis and Human Evolution," in *Oxford Research Encyclopedia of Psychology* (March 2016), http://dx.doi.org/10.1093/acreforc/9780190236557.013.44.

5. See, generally, David D. Gilmore, *Manhood in the Making: Cultural Concepts of Masculinity* (New Haven, CT: Yale University Press, 1990).

6. Ryan, *Civilized to Death.*

Preface

1. See these media appearances by Ed Adams: "Michael Discusses Toxic Masculinity with Dr. Edward M. Adams," interview by

Michael Strahan, *Good Morning America*, January 23, 2019, https://www.goodmorningamerica.com/gma_day/video/michael-discusses-toxic-masculinity-dr-edward-adams-60573623; "Traditional Masculinity Under Attack," Edward M. Adams interviewed by Laura Ingraham, *The Ingraham Angle*, January 14, 2019, https://www.youtube.com/watch?v=iYJhfZ9Ad4U; "Is There Such a Thing As Toxic Masculinity?," Edward M. Adams and Allie Stuckey interviewed by Todd Starnes, *Fox News*, January 15, 2019, https://video.foxnews.com/v/5989711340001/#sp=show-clips; "The APA's New Guidelines for Men and Boys," Edward M. Adams and Matt Englar-Carlson interviewed by Alison Stewart, *All of It*, WNYC, February 15, 2019, https://www.wnyc.org/story/apas-new-guidelines-men-boys/; Ed Adams, contributor, The Good Men Project, "The Healing Power of Compassion in Men's Lives," *HuffPost*, September 13, 2015; updated December 6, 2017, https://www.huffpost.com/entry/the-healing-power-of-compassion-in-mens-lives_b_8033430; and Thomas B. Edsall, "The Fight over Men Is Shaping Our Political Future," *The New York Times*, January 17, 2019, https://www.nytimes.com/2019/01/17/opinion/apa-guidelines-men-boys.html.

2. Michael C. Bush and the Great Place to Work Research Team, *A Great Place to Work for All: Better for Business, Better for People, Better for the World* (Oakland, CA: Berrett-Koehler Publishers, 2018), https://www.greatplacetowork.com/book.

3. Ed Frauenheim, "Losing Our Way: How Worrying Too Much about Winning Derailed Me—And Puts All of Us off Course," *Medium*, February 10, 2018, https://medium.com/@edfrauenheim/losing-our-way-a0a107d94aa8.

Introduction

1. Ella Koeze and Anna Maria Barry-Jester, "What Do Men Think It Means to Be a Man?" *FiveThirtyEight*, June 20, 2018, https://fivethirtyeight.com/features/what-do-men-think-it-means-to-be-a-man/.

2. American Psychological Association, "APA Guidelines for Psychological Practice with Boys and Men," August 2018, https:// www.apa.org/about/policy/boys-men-practice-guidelines.pdf.

3. See U.S. Centers for Disease Control and Prevention, Suicide: Facts at a Glance 2015, https://www.cdc.gov/violenceprevention/pdf/ suicide-datasheet-a.pdf; and American Psychological Association, "By the Numbers: Men and Depression," *Monitor on Psychology* 46, no. 11 (December 2015): 13, https://www.apa.org/monitor/2015/12 /numbers. The figure of 30.6 percent of men suffering from a period of depression in their lifetime involves measurement with a "gender inclusive depression scale" that includes symptoms such as rage and risk-taking.

4. Shana Lynch, "Why Your Workplace Might Be Killing You," *Insights by Stanford Business*, February 23, 2015, https://www .gsb.stanford.edu/insights/why-your-workplace-might-be-killing -you; and Ed Frauenheim, "Giving Thanks for a Great Workplace," *Great Place to Work* (blog), November 21, 2018, https://www .greatplacetowork.com/resources/blog/giving-thanks-for-a-great -workplace.

5. Aja Romano, "How the Alt-Right's Sexism Lures Men into White Supremacy," *Vox*, updated April 26, 2018, https://www.vox .com/culture/2016/12/14/13576192/alt-right-sexism-recruitment.

6. Ken Wilber, "Foreword" in *Reinventing Organizations: A Guide to Creating Organizations Inspired by the Next Stage of Human Consciousness* (Brussels: Nelson Parker, 2014), ix–x.

Chapter 1

1. Richard Godbeer, *The Overflowing of Friendship: Love Between Men and the Creation of the American Republic* (Baltimore: Johns Hopkins University Press, 2009), 164.

2. Brian Ogawa, *A River to Live By: The 12 Life Principles of Morita Therapy* (Philadelphia: Xlibris, 2007), 127–28.

3. Stephanie Pappas, "APA Issues First-Ever Guidelines for Practice with Men and Boys," *Monitor on Psychology* 50, no. 1, (2019): 34, American Psychological Association, https://www.apa.org /monitor/2019/01/ce-corner.

4. Robert Brannon, "The Male Sex Role—and What It's Done for Us Lately," in *The Forty-Nine Percent Majority,* eds. Debra S. David and Robert Brannon (Reading, MA: Addison Wesley, 1976), 1–40.

5. We'd like to add a caveat to the notion that recorded history has been marked by a male ethos of domination, stoicism, and sexism. While that is generally true, there has been great diversity in the way men have defined themselves in both Western and Eastern civilizations. Men haven't always conformed to a rigid version of confined masculinity over the past 6,000 years, or so.

6. Author Christopher Ryan sums up much of the research on foraging groups in his 2019 book, *Civilized to Death: The Price of Progress.* He notes that hunter-gatherer societies tend to feature relative equality between men and women; see Ryan, *Civilized to Death: The Price of Progress* (New York: Avid Reader Press/Simon & Schuster, 2019), 60.

7. Ken Wilber, *A Brief History of Everything* (Boston: Shambhala, 1996), 48–52.

8. See Paul Gilbert's foreword to this book. Christopher Ryan is among those who question whether farming and the rise of nations amounted to true progress for men and women. "If you...were hoping for an egalitarian world of shared plenitude and lots of free time to enjoy the company of those you love, consider that our ancestors enjoyed a world very much like that until the advent of agriculture and what came to be called 'civilization' sprouted about ten thousand years ago." Ryan, *Civilized to Death,* 8.

9. Robert M. Sapolsky, *The Trouble with Testosterone: And Other Essays on the Biology of the Human Predicament* (New York: Touchstone, 1997), 151–52.

10. Robert M. Sapolsky and Lisa J. Share, "A Pacific Culture among Wild Baboons: Its Emergence and Transmission," *PLoS*

Biology 2, no. 4 (April 2004): 534–41, https://journals.plos.org /plosbiology/article/file?type=printable&id=10.1371/journal.pbio .0020106.

11. Janet Shibley Hyde, "The Gender Similarities Hypothesis," *American Psychologist* 60, no. 6 (September 2005): 581–92, https:// www.apa.org/pubs/journals/releases/amp-606581.pdf; and American Psychological Association, "Men and Women: No Big Difference," *Research in Action*, October 20, 2005, https://www.apa.org/research /action/difference.

Chapter 2

1. Brian Ogawa, *A River to Live By: The 12 Life Principles of Morita Therapy* (Philadelphia: Xlibris, 2007).

2. "Striving for Ubuntu," Desmond Tutu Peace Foundation, October 6, 2015, http://www.tutufoundationusa.org/2015/10/06 /striving-for-ubuntu/.

3. Geshe Kelsang Gyatso, *Modern Buddhism: The Path of Compassion and Wisdom*, vol. 1, 2d ed. (Glen Spey, NY: Tharpa Publications, 2015), 83.

4. Gyatso, *Modern Buddhism*, 74–81.

5. Rainer Maria Rilke, *Letters to a Young Poet*, rev. ed. (New York: W. W. Norton, 1993), 41.

Chapter 3

1. Ed Frauenheim, "How Edward Jones Keeps Its Employees Happy to Come to Work," *Fortune*, March 27, 2018, https://fortune .com/2018/03/27/edward-jones-best-company-finance-happy -workers/.

2. Marilee Adams, *Change Your Questions, Change Your Life: 12 Powerful Tools for Leadership, Coaching, and Life*, 3rd. ed. (Oakland: Berrett-Koehler Publishers, 2016); for the Choice Map visit https:// inquiry-institute.myshopify.com/collections/frontpage/products /cm-dl.

3. Kyle Buchanan, "The Planets, the Stars and Brad Pitt," *The New York Times*, updated September 8, 2019, https://www.nytimes.com/2019/09/04/movies/brad-pitt-ad-astra.html.

4. Brené Brown, quoted in Peter Economy, "17 Brené Brown Quotes to Inspire You to Success and Happiness," *Inc.*, January 8, 2016, https://www.inc.com/peter-economy/17-brene-brown-quotes-to-inspire-you-to-success-and-happiness.html.

5. Ed Frauenheim, "My Son Laps Me," *Medium*, November 30, 2018, https://medium.com/@cdfrauenheim/my-son-laps-me-ca5ebea284bf.

6. Emily Tate, "Why Social-Emotional Learning Is Suddenly in the Spotlight," *EdSurge Podcast*, May 7, 2019, https://www.edsurge.com/news/2019-05-07-why-social-emotional-learning-is-suddenly-in-the-spotlight.

7. Tony Bond, "High-Trust Culture Consulting," Great Place to Work Annual Conference, June 27, 2017, https://www.youtube.com/watch?v=2euRJyCJkn8&t=4s.

Chapter 4

1. Personal communication with Paul Gilbert. See also the foreword of this book and Paul Gilbert, *Living Like Crazy* (York, U.K.: Annwyn House, 2018).

2. Emma Seppälä, "Are Women Really More Compassionate?" EmmaSeppala.com, June 20, 2013, https://emmaseppala.com/are-women-really-more-compassionate.

3. Kristin Neff, cited in Lisa Firestone, "The Many Benefits of Self-Compassion," *Psychology Today*, October 29, 2016, https://www.psychologytoday.com/us/blog/compassion-matters/201610/the-many-benefits-self-compassion. See also Kristen Neff's TEDx talk on "The Space Between Self-Esteem and Self-Compassion," February 7, 2013, https://www.youtube.com/watch?v=IvtZBUSplr4.

4. Ronald F. Levant, "Desperately Seeking Language: Understanding, Assessing and Treating Normative Male Alexithymia," in *The New Handbook of Counseling and Psychotherapy for Men: A*

Comprehensive Guide to Settings, Problems, and Treatment Approaches,
vol. 1, eds. Glenn E. Good and Gary R. Brooks (San Francisco:
Jossey-Bass, 2001), 424–43.

Chapter 5

1. Vivek Murthy, "Work and the Loneliness Epidemic,"
Harvard Business Review, September 27, 2017, https://hbr.org/cover
-story/2017/09/work-and-the-loneliness-epidemic.

2. See Jane E. Brody, "The Challenges of Male Friendships," *New
York Times,* June 27, 2016, https://well.blogs.nytimes.com/2016/06/27
/the-challenges-of-male-friendships/.

3. Andrew L. Yarrow, "All the Lonely Men," *Baltimore Sun,*
October 19, 2018, https://www.baltimoresun.com/opinion/op-ed/bs
-ed-op-1021-lonley-men-20181018-story.html.

4. Daniel Goleman, Richard Boyatzis, and Annie McKee, *Primal
Leadership: Learning to Lead with Emotional Intelligence* (Boston:
Harvard Business Review Press, 2013), 7.

5. Brené Brown, "The Power of Vulnerability," filmed June 2010,
TEDxHouston video, 20:04, www.ted.com/talks/brene_brown_the
_power_of_vulnerability.

6. Godbeer, *The Overflowing of Friendship: Love Between Men
and the Creation of the American Republic* (Baltimore: Johns Hopkins
University Press, 2009), 193, 4.

7. Interview with Dusty Araujo, conducted by Ed Frauenheim,
December 7, 2019.

8. Araujo interview, December 7, 2019.

Chapter 6

1. Michael C. Bush and the Great Place to Work Research Team,
*A Great Place to Work for All: Better for Business, Better for People, Better
for the World* (Oakland: Berrett-Koehler, 2018).

2. Studs Terkel, *Working: People Talk about What They Do All Day
and How They Feel about What They Do* (New York: New Press, 1997), xi.

3. Ed Frauenheim, "The Great Workplace Era Emerges in Asia," Great Place to Work Institute Blog, March 13, 2015, https://www .greatplacetowork.com/resources/blog/the-great-workplace-era -emerges-in-asia.

4. Ed Frauenheim and Great Place to Work, "How the 150 Best Medium and Small Workplaces Race Ahead," *Fortune*, October 18, 2018, https://fortune.com/2018/10/18/150-best-medium-small -workplaces-2018/.

5. The Police, "Synchronicity II," from *Synchronicity*, A&M Records, 1983.

6. See Jim Harter, "4 Factors Driving Record-High Employee Engagement in U.S.," Gallup *Workplace*, February 4, 2020, https:// www.gallup.com/workplace/284180/factors-driving-record-high -employee-engagement.aspx; and Jim Harter, "Dismal Employee Engagement Is a Sign of Global Mismanagement," Gallup Blog, n.d., accessed April 10, 2020, https://www.gallup.com/workplace/231668 /dismal-employee-engagement-sign-global-mismanagement.aspx. Survey organization Gallup found in 2019 that 35 percent of U.S. employees were engaged—meaning they are "highly involved in, enthusiastic about, and committed to their work and workplace." That represented the highest level since Gallup began tracking the statistic in 2000, when engagement stood at 26 percent. The progress may reflect changes in the business world in keeping with a liberating masculinity. But the fact that, despite the improvement, only about one-third of employees were engaged in 2019 is telling. It signals how far our organizations have to go to be places where all people thrive, and is an indictment of confined masculinity as a management model.

7. The term "deadening" isn't just figurative. Our workplaces— informed by a confined masculinity model of management—literally kill people. In the United States, relatively few of those deaths are from workplace accidents directly. Instead, they come mostly from stressful, toxic work environments. Research from Stanford and Harvard business schools shows "health problems stemming from

job stress, like hypertension, cardiovascular disease, and decreased mental health, can lead to fatal conditions that wind up killing about 120,000 people each year." See Gillian B. White, "The Alarming, Long-Term Consequences of Workplace Stress," *Atlantic*, February 12, 2015, https://www.theatlantic.com/business/archive/2015/02/the -alarming-long-term-consequences-of-workplace-stress/385397/, and Stephanie Denning, "How Stress Is the Business World's Silent Killer," *Forbes*, May 4, 2018, https://www.forbes.com/sites/ stephaniedenning/2018/05/04/what-is-the-cost-of-stress-how-stress -is-the-business-worlds-silent-killer/#71f7d4986e06. Among the causes of that job stress are factors directly tied to hyper-masculine-flavored management: lack of power over one's job (reflects the domination of power by leaders), the inability to balance work and family conflicts (reflects indifference to emotional ties beyond work), and long hours (reflects an unwillingness to tolerate or show weakness).

8. See Dov Seidman, "From the Knowledge Economy to the Human Economy," *Harvard Business Review*, November 12, 2014, https://hbr.org/2014/11/from-the-knowledge-economy-to-the -human-economy.

9. John T. Chambers, the long-time CEO of technology giant Cisco Systems, says companies will not be able to succeed if they wait for senior executives to learn about problems and make decisions—especially as more and more data streams flow into organizations. "You're going to have information coming into your company in ways you never imagined before," Chambers says. "Decisions will be made much further down in the organization at a fast pace." See Michael C. Bush and the Great Place to Work Research Team, *A Great Place to Work for All: Better for Business, Better for People, Better for the World* (Oakland, CA: Berrett-Koehler Publishers, 2018), 2. https://www .greatplacetowork.com/book.

10. Marcus Erb, Jessica Rohman, Ed Frauenheim, Chandni Kazi, and Nancy Ceseña, "Innovation by All: The New Flight Plan for Elevating Ingenuity, Accelerating Performance, and Outpacing

Rivals," Great Place to Work, 2018, http://learn.greatplacetowork
.com/rs/520-AOO-982/images/2018_innovation_by_all_FINAL.pdf.

11. Ed Frauenheim, "From Man of Steel to Men of Teal: A New
Vision of Male Leadership," LinkedIn Pulse Blog, June 14, 2019,
https://www.linkedin.com/pulse/from-man-steel-men-teal-new
-vision-male-leadership-ed-frauenheim/.

12. Julia Rozovsky, "The Five Keys to a Successful Google Team,"
re:Work, November 17, 2015, https://rework.withgoogle.com/blog
/five-keys-to-a-successful-google-team/.

13. Ed Frauenheim and Shawn Murphy, "Caring as a Competitive
Advantage," Great Place to Work Blog, January 13, 2017, https://
www.greatplacetowork.com/resources/blog/caring-as-competitive
-weapon.

14. See, for example, Marshall Goldsmith with Mark Reiter, *What
Got You Here Won't Get You There: How Successful People Become Even
More Successful* (New York: Hachette, 2007).

15. Adam Grant, *Give and Take: Why Helping Others Drives Our
Success* (New York: Penguin Books, 2014), 10. Grant notes that there's
a shadow side of a "giving" style of interaction. Givers tend to be
concentrated at the extremes of the success scale—not only at the
top but at the bottom. They end up among the lowest in measures of
success, Grant notes, because others often take advantage of them.

16. See Ed Frauenheim, "Elon Musk, 'Atlas CEOs,' and
Rehumanizing Leadership," LinkedIn Pulse Blog, August 29,
2018, https://www.linkedin.com/pulse/elon-musk-atlas-ceos-re
-humanizing-leadership-ed-frauenheim/.

17. Richard Henderson, "Industry Employment and Output
Projections to 2024," *Monthly Labor Review*, U.S. Bureau of Labor
Statistics, December 2015, https://doi.org/10.21916/mlr.2015.47.

18. Linnea Engström, "Climate Change Is a Feminist Issue,"
Friends of Europe, April 11, 2017, https://www.friendsofeurope.org
/insights/climate-change-is-a-feminist-issue/; and Matthew Ballew,
Jennifer Marlon, Anthony Leiserowitz, and Edward Maibach,

"Gender Differences in Public Understanding of Climate Change," *Yale Program on Climate Change Communication*, November 20, 2018, https://climatecommunication.yale.edu/publications/gender-differences-in-public-understanding-of-climate-change/.

19. Ed Frauenheim, "How the World's Best Workplaces Create a Great Global Culture," *Fortune*, October 2, 2019, https://fortune.com/2019/10/02/worlds-best-workplaces-global-culture/.

20. Business Roundtable, "Business Roundtable Redefines the Purpose of a Corporation to Promote 'An Economy That Serves All Americans,'" August 19, 2019, https://www.businessroundtable.org/business-roundtable-redefines-the-purpose-of-a-corporation-to-promote-an-economy-that-serves-all-americans.

21. Conscious Capitalism, accessed March 4, 2020, https://www.consciouscapitalism.org/.

22. Frederic Laloux, *Reinventing Organizations: A Guide to Creating Organizations Inspired by the Next Stage of Human Consciousness* (Brussels: Nelson Parker, 2014), 48.

23. Laloux, *Reinventing Organizations*.

24. Ed Frauenheim, "From Man of Steel to Men of Teal."

25. Brent Lowe, Susan Basterfield, and Travis Marsh, *Reinventing Scale-Ups: Radical Ideas for Growing Companies* (San Francisco: ReinventingScaleUps.com, 2017).

26. For more on the Teal Team, please visit https://thetealteam.com/.

Chapter 7

1. Donald Richie, *A Tractate on Japanese Aesthetics* (Berkeley: Stone Bridge Press, 2007), 57.

2. James Hillman, *The Soul's Code: In Search of Character and Calling* (New York: Random House), 1996, 4–14.

3. Ken Wilber, "Foreword" in *Reinventing Organizations: A Guide to Creating Organizations Inspired by the Next Stage of Human Consciousness* (Brussels: Nelson Parker, 2014), ix–x.

4. Matthew Fox, *The Hidden Spirituality of Men: Ten Metaphors to Awaken the Sacred Masculine* (Novato, CA: New World Library, 2009), xxvii.

Conclusion

1. Dalai Lama, *The Art of Happiness* (New York: Riverhead Books, 2009), 129.

2. Matthew D. Lieberman, *Social: Why Our Brains Are Wired to Connect* (New York: Broadway Books, 2013), 250.

3. Holly Barlow Sweet, ed., *Gender in the Therapy Hour: Voices of Female Clinicians Working with Men* (New York: Routledge, 2012), 9–10.

4. Practicing gratitude is associated with improved mental health. See "Gratitude Is Good Medicine," UC Davis Health blog, November 25, 2015, https://health.ucdavis.edu/medicalcenter /features/2015-2016/11/20151125_gratitude.html.

RESOURCES

Discussion Guide

The following twelve questions are intended for men to ponder and discuss in groups:

1. On a personal level, what does it mean for you to be a man?

2. Identify a man who had a strong influence in your life. What did this man teach you about being a man?

3. What rules of manhood have you abided by? How did you learn these rules?

4. What brings out compassion in you? Why might you withhold compassion?

5. How hard is it for you to build and maintain close friendships? Why do you think many men are isolated?

6. Think about the women in your life. What kind of man do they seem to want you to be or become? How do their expectations affect you ?

7. How can men expand their circle of care and compassion? How might this expansion make the world a better place?

8. Do you practice self-compassion? If so, how? How can men help each other to develop self-compassion skills?

9. How have you seen confined masculinity show up at work? How have you seen liberating masculinity show up at work?

10. Do you notice growing expectations at work for men to be flexible, warm, and connected? Do you feel emotionally safe at work? Please explain your responses.

11. How frequently do you express your strong emotions to others? What gets in the way of being that expressive?

12. Can you describe a life experience that touched your very soul? How might being a soulful man enrich your life?

Reinventing Masculinity Self-Assessment

On each of the following items, circle the number that most accurately reflects your experience.

Question	Strongly Disagree ———		Neutral	———	Strongly Agree
I identify my feelings and express my feelings.	1	2	3	4	5
I practice self-compassion by not beating myself up.	1	2	3	4	5
I have close and connected male friends.	1	2	3	4	5
I ask for emotional support from others.	1	2	3	4	5
I enjoy cooperating as much as or more than competing.	1	2	3	4	5
I often challenge traditional man-rules.	1	2	3	4	5
My soul or inner spirit feels open and alive.	1	2	3	4	5
I am comfortable with people who are different from me.	1	2	3	4	5
I feel connected to all people and all living beings.	1	2	3	4	5
I view women and people with diverse sexual identities as equals.	1	2	3	4	5

Add up your responses. If you're total score is:

10–16: RED. It's time to stop. Reflect on your behaviors and question your beliefs about masculinity. What first step can you take that moves you toward liberating masculinity?

17–33: YELLOW. Caution: be aware that, from here, you could go either way. Choose the road toward liberating masculinity.

34–50: GREEN. Proceed—continue on your way toward liberating masculinity, and help others on their journey.

Places to Connect, Things to Do, Resources to Explore

Places to Connect

American Men's Studies Association: "Advancing the critical study of men and masculinities." https://mensstudies.org/

American Psychological Association: "Advancing psychology to benefit society and improve lives." https://www.apa.org/

Better Man Conference: "An event with resources, support, and community to engage men as allies in creating an inclusive culture." https://bettermanconference.com/

The Good Men Project: "An international conversation about what it means to be a good man in the twenty-first century." https://goodmenproject.com/

HealthDirect: an Australia-based resource with mental health resources for men. https://www.healthdirect.gov.au/mens-mental-health

Health Disparities Institute at the University of Connecticut: Seeks "to reduce disparities by turning ideas shown to work into policies and actions"—especially to eliminate injustices suffered by boys and men of color. https://health.uconn.edu/health-disparities/

Mankind Project: "A not-for-profit international training and educational organization." https://mankindproject.org/

Men Mentoring Men (M3): "A self-sustaining council of thoughtful men dedicated to participation in and appreciation of the triumphs and failures of life's journey by enriching the lives of each other, those we love, and the community at large." https://www.MenMentoringMen.org

Men's Health Network: "A national nonprofit organization whose mission is to reach men, boys, and their families where they live, work, play, and pray with health awareness and disease prevention messages and tools, screening programs, educational materials, advocacy opportunities, and patient navigation." http://www.mens healthnetwork.org/

Men's Resource Center for Change: "Supporting men, challenging men's violence, and developing men's leadership in ending oppression in our lives, our families, and our communities." https://www.mensresourcecenter.org/

Men's Suicide Prevention Resource Center. https://www.sprc.org/populations/men

National Institute of Mental Health: "Real Men—Real Depression Campaign." https://www.nimh.nih.gov/health/topics/men-and-mental-health/men-and-depression/nimhs-real-men-real-depression-campaign.shtml

National Organization for Men Against Sexism: "An activist organization of men and women supporting positive changes for men....We affirm that working to make this nation's ideals of equality substantive is the finest expression of what it means to be men." https://nomas.org/

Society for the Psychological Study of Men and Masculinities, Division 51 of the American Psychological Association. https://www.division51.net

The Violence Prevention Alliance (VPA): "A network of WHO member states, international agencies, and civil society organizations working to prevent violence." https://www.who.int/violenceprevention/

Things to Do

Get together with a few men to discuss your ideas about what it means to be a man. Start with the twelve questions in the Discussion Guide above. Continue with the questions posed throughout this book.

Introduce a conversation about men and masculinity with someone you care about. Tell them about a man who influenced your attitudes about masculinity.

Make a list of men you admire and respect. Describe their qualities, and why they inspire you. Can you interview one?

Search for a men's group in your community. Religious centers, mental health providers, and community centers are good places to start. Or, since healthy men's groups are hard to find, consider starting one—it takes only two men to start a discussion. Let it grow organically.

Encourage your local bookstore to carry more books about men's physical and emotional health. Men's issues are often seen as not important, or bookstore managers may believe that men don't buy books. If it's a tough sell, consider hosting a bookstore panel discussing men's issues.

Visit your primary physician for an annual check-up. Men underutilize health services of all kinds. Be the exception.

If you're thinking about getting counseling, go for it! Find a therapist with experience treating men. Search online, or ask others if they know a good therapist.

If you are a parent, talk to your children about men and masculinity. Encourage your kids to feel pride about their gender.

Be generous. Give some of your time, energy, and money to causes that make the world a better place. Take direct action by helping others or our environment.

When socializing with others, begin a discussion about liberating masculinity.

Resources to Explore

Adams, Edward M. *Becoming a Happier Man: A Man's Guide to Living a Full and Meaningful Life.* Pennsauken, NJ: BookBaby, 2017. https://www.amazon.com/Becoming-Happier-Man-Living-Meaningful/dp/1483588289.

Adams, Edward M., contributor, The Good Men Project. "The Healing Power of Compassion in Men's Lives." *HuffPost*, updated December 6, 2017. https://www.huffpost.com/entry/the-healing-power-of-compassion-in-mens-lives_b_8033430.

Brooks, Gary R. *Beyond the Crisis of Masculinity: A Transtheoretical Model for Male-Friendly Therapy.* Washington, DC: American Psychological Association, 2010. https://www.amazon.com/Beyond-Crisis-Masculinity-Transtheoretical-Male-Friendly/dp/1433807165.

Bush, Michael C., and the Great Place to Work Research Team. *A Great Place to Work for All: Better for Business, Better for People, Better for the World.* Oakland, CA: Berrett-Koehler Publishers, 2018. https://www.greatplacetowork.com/book.

Englar-Carlson, Matt, and Mark A. Stevens, editors. *In the Room with Men: A Casebook of Therapeutic Change.* Washington, DC: American Psychological Association, 2006. https://www.amazon.com/Room-Men-Casebook-Therapeutic-Change/dp/1591473322.

Frauenheim, Ed. "From Man of Steel to Men of Teal: A New Vision of Male Leadership." LinkedIn Blog, June 14, 2019. https://www.linkedin.com/pulse/from-man-steel-men-teal-new-vision-male-leadership-ed-frauenheim/.

Gilbert, Paul, editor. *Compassion: Concepts, Research and Applications.* New York: Routledge, 2017. https://www.amazon.com/gp/product/1138957194.

Gilbert, Paul. *Mindful Compassion: How the Science of Compassion Can Help You Understand Your Emotions, Live in the Present, and Connect Deeply with Others.* Oakland: New Harbinger, 2014. https://

www.amazon.com/Mindful-Compassion-Science-Understand
-Emotions/dp/1626250618.

Horowitz, Richard. *Walk Like a Man: Redefining Masculinity for a Modern World* (blog). http://oktobeaman.com/.

Laloux, Frederic. *Reinventing Organizations: A Guide to Creating Organizations Inspired by the Next Stage of Human Consciousness.* Brussels: Nelson Parker, 2014. https://www.amazon.com /Reinventing-Organizations-Frederic-Laloux/dp/2960133501/.

Levant, Ronald F. *Masculinity Reconstructed: Changing the Rules of Manhood—At Work, in Relationships, and in Family Life.* New York: Plume, 1996. https://www.amazon.com/Masculinity -Reconstructed-Changing-Manhood-at-Relationships /dp/052593846X/.

Lieberman, Matthew D. *Social: Why Our Brains Are Wired to Connect.* New York: Broadway Books, 2013. https://www.amazon.com /Social-Why-Brains-Wired-Connect/dp/0307889106/.

Lomas, Tim. *Masculinity, Meditation and Mental Health.* New York: Palgrave Macmillan, 2014. https://www.amazon.com/Masculinity -Meditation-Mental-Health-Lomas-dp-1349466379/dp/13494 66379/.

Neff, Kristin. *Self-Compassion: The Proven Power of Being Kind to Yourself.* New York: William Morrow, 2011. https://www.amazon .com/Self-Compassion-Proven-Power-Being-Yourself/dp/B005 SA69UM/.

Ogawa, Brian. *Desire for Life: The Practitioner's Introduction to Morita Therapy for the Treatment of Anxiety Disorders.* Bloomington, IN: Xlibris, 2013. https://www.amazon.com/Desire-Life-Practitioners -Introduction-Treatment/dp/1483604470/.

Rabinowitz, Fredric E. *Deepening Group Psychotherapy With Men: Stories and Insights for the Journey.* Washington, DC: American Psychological Association, 2001. https://www.amazon.com /Deepening-Group-Psychotherapy-Men-Insights/dp/1433829444/.

Sapolsky, Robert M. *The Trouble with Testosterone: And Other Essays on the Biology of the Human Predicament.* New York: Touchstone,

1997). https://www.amazon.com/Trouble-Testosterone-Essays
-Biology-Predicament/dp/0684838915/.

Smiler, Andrew. *Is Masculinity Toxic? A Primer for the 21st Century.*
New York: Thames & Hudson, 2019. https://www.amazon.com
/Masculinity-Toxic-Primer-21st-Century/dp/0500295026.

Wexler, David B. *When Good Men Behave Badly: Change Your
Behavior, Change Your Relationship.* Oakland: New Harbinger
Press, 2004. https://www.amazon.com/When-Good-Men-Behave
-Badly-ebook/dp/B0073SV92A. 6

ACKNOWLEDGMENTS

This book is the product of many people, who supported us in many different ways.

To start with, we want to thank our editor Steve Piersanti, founder of Berrett-Koehler Publishers. Steve trusted us to create a worthy book, then kept giving us encouragement as well as sage advice to make it better. We also thank the broader BK team that has made *Reinventing Masculinity* possible, sometimes through candid and even hard-to-hear feedback. This appreciation extends to Kirsten Janene-Nelson for her thoughtful edits.

One of the great things about BK is its extended community—a community of authors, readers, reviewers, and activists dedicated to creating a world that works for all. We're grateful to that bigger BK circle as well. A special shout out to fellow BK author Marilee Adams, who put us Eds together initially, believing that we'd find a way to make two Eds better than one.

We also want to make some individual acknowledgments.

Edward M. Adams, PsyD

No worthy project is ever accomplished alone and this book is no exception.

Marilee Adams, my wife, is also my anchor and champion. I am a lucky man to love and be loved by such a smart, beautiful, and wise woman. With Marilee's abiding care and respect, my heart doesn't just tick—it dances through life.

My relationship with my son, David Zachary Adams, has given me the experience of father love. But it should be known that Zak makes it easy to love him. Thank you for teaching me how connected a father can feel toward his son.

My immediate family has been the cornerstone of my life. Ed and Rose Adams ignited compassion in my soul and taught me the value of connecting with a purpose beyond myself. My sisters, Kathy Inglert and Robin Richardson, are continuous sources of love and pride. And thank you for bringing Laura, Emily, Deanna, Shane, and Mark into my life.

Then, there are all the men in my life; men I met in friendship and men I had the privilege to help in therapy. Men who mentored and believed in me and even men who inflicted wounds. What I know about masculinities has much to do with you. A special thank you to Rutgers University, Paul Gilbert for his courage and pioneering work on compassion, and to Gen Wangden, a Buddhist monk whose teaching of Dharma opened many doors for my soul to enter.

I am indebted to the men and women within my home in the American Psychological Association's Division 51. This division is small but mighty. And it uses its might to help make the world a better place for men and women to live and grow. I thank those who had the vision to start Division 51 and those who work hard every day to sustain that vision. Some of these men and women include Mike Andronico, Larry Beer, Tyler Bradstreet, Gary Brooks, Cary Cherniss, Brian Cole, Jon Davies, Will Elder, Bill Johnson, Dick Kessler, Chris Kilmartin, Mark Kiselica, Chris Kotsen, Ron Levant, Chris Liang, Judith Logue, Neil Massoth, Ryon McDermott, Fred Rabinowitz, Christopher Reigeluth, David Shepard, Dan Singley, Andrew Smiler, and Jay Wade. I worked closely with Holly Barlow Sweet, Daniel Ellenberg, Michele Harway, Ryan McKelley, Michael Parent, Wizdom Powell, Randa Remer-Eskridge, and David Whitcomb. You and everyone else within the division positively influenced my tenure as president and helped deepen my understanding of men and masculinities.

I am particularly grateful to the men involved with Men Mentoring Men (M3) over the past thirty years. You are some of the most courageous, dedicated, and visionary men I will ever have the pleasure to call friends—period. I have always felt honored and inspired by your belief in the core values of M3. These values focus on courage, compassion, and connection. You are living proof of the power of men to upgrade the man-rules. And there are times when you actually listened to me no matter how challenging or confronting a request. Please know two important things. First, you make our world a better place to live. Second, you represent the best of what men are about.

There are so many individual men of M3 to appreciate, too many to mention because the list keeps growing. But I want

ACKNOWLEDGMENTS

to thank the men who signed on to M3 in its early stage and enabled it grow, the men who serve as executive board members, and each of the present and past presidents and group leaders. These men volunteer their wisdom and love to help other men move toward and sustain a more generous and caring manhood.

I want to honor my writing partner, Ed Frauenheim. You are a kind, smart, insightful, and loving man with strong writing skills. I deeply respect your desire for men and women to wake up and do something to make our world a safer and more loving place. You are a man with a deep soul.

Finally, thank you, our readers, for caring about men and liberating masculinities. The only way things will improve in our crazy world is for good people to join forces and reclaim compassion as a force of life—as well as to offer kindness and love to sustain it.

Ed Frauenheim

I thank my father, Edward E. Frauenheim III, for showing me an unconventional, always-curious, loving kind of manhood, and for remaining a great support to me. This book also owes a lot to my deceased mom, Marty Frauenheim. She not only helped me believe in myself, but modeled kind-and-firm leadership in her professional life that blended the best "feminine" and "masculine" traits.

In addition, I'm grateful for my brother and sister. Kirk Frauenheim is one of the finest men you could meet, and Kate Criddle is one of the wisest souls I know.

Close male friends have been on this journey toward a liberating masculinity with me. They live in these pages: Raúl

Ramos, Jason Patent, Paul Rudnick, Joel Zarrow, Art Bender, and David Balsley.

I also thank my "men-in-laws" for modeling positive versions of masculinity: Carl Richie, Carty Richie, Steve Richie, and Daniel Criddle.

A range of other people and communities have carried me through this process or made important contributions. They include my Teal Team peeps: Newt Bailey, Marcus Erb, Julia Markish, Travis Marsh, Jay Newman, Valerie Rivera, Matt Spaur, and Paul Thallner. Also vital were my Fighting Snakessss pals Teresa Iafolla and Jessica Rohman. My writing group, the Heralds, has lifted me up and shaken sense into my words for years: Erin Albert, Monique Beeler, Leslie Mladinich, and Rachel Roberson.

I also had great support from my colleagues at Great Place to Work. A special shout out to Michael C. Bush, Ann Nadeau, and Chris Tkaczyk for enabling me to pursue this book. And to my content cronies Nancy Ceseña, Chandni Kazi, Tony Bond, Sarah Lewis-Kulin, Julian Lute, Lorena Martinez, Julie Musilek, Tabitha Russell Wilhelmsen, Lizelle Festejo Hsu, Cessi Riva Mosquera, Otto Zell, Jamie Dowden, Kristen McCammon, Erika Richardson Koh, and Tessa Herns (and Marcus again) for the partnership and the research findings we've made that show we need to reinvent masculinity at work.

Temple Crocker, Alan Briskin, Maren Showkeir, Kanu Kogod, Michelle Rafter, Mary Egan, David Ferris, Samantha Slade, Paul Messer, Jennifer Kahnweiler, Libby Bestul, Colette Plum, Helen Nadel, Laura Kelly, Sara Jansen Perry, Courtney Hanny, Josh Goldfein, Maggi Henderson, Dusty

Araujo, Paul Wright, David Marshall, Laurie Bassi, Dan McMurrer, Wendy Cai and the Maxfield's crew, Charu Rachlis, Stephanie Snyder, and Jason Bowman all get credit for feeding my head, touching my heart, or guiding my hands—sometimes all three.

I have great appreciation for my coauthor, Ed Adams. Ed taught me so much about men, the common challenges we face, and the possibilities open to us. I'm grateful for all the good he has done in his work over many years, for his artistic additions to this book, and for his caring collaboration overall.

My greatest thanks come last. I am grateful to my son, Julius, and my daughter, Skyla. These two teens keep teaching me about a better masculinity. And I thank my wife, Rowena Richie. She had my back on this project, and for two decades she has helped me become ever-freer as a man.

We're sure we've left out important people. Please forgive those omissions. And while the people mentioned above deserve credit if this book moves you, it's not their fault if it doesn't. That would be on us.

Edward M. Adams and
Ed Frauenheim

INDEX

ABOUT THE AUTHORS

Dr. Ed Adams After earning his doctor of psychology degree from Rutgers University, Ed Adams began a private practice in psychology. Years later, Ed recognized a need to reinvent his life. As a consequence, he left that group practice to pursue a coexisting career in painting and sculpture. People were dismayed that he would leave a thriving psychological practice to "become an artist." Some believed Ed was "nuts" for making that decision or "irresponsible" to pursue a dream without assurance of a good income from his art. But in time, he opened his own art gallery to show and sell his works of art.

Today, Ed's work is in collections worldwide, including at Rutgers University and Hebrew University in Israel; Steven Spielberg owns one of his sculptures. Looking back, Ed reports that the science and art of psychology and the art of making images are intertwined and have brought him deep fulfillment.

In fact, now, three decades later, Ed shudders at the thought of not having listened to those creative longings within his soul. He understands that the thread that ties everything together for him is creativity. Psychotherapy is creative. Art is creative. Indeed, becoming more fully human is creative.

Over the past decades, the art of psychotherapy with individual men, Ed's presidency of Division 51 (Men and Masculinities) of the American Psychological Association (APA), and the founding of Men Mentoring Men (M3) have focused his creative interests toward assisting other men to build more satisfying and meaningful lives. Ed found a way to do this by blending psychology with art.

Ed's first book, *Becoming a Happier Man: A Man's Guide to Living a Full and Meaningful Life* (BookBaby, 2017) identifies the elements present when a man can say, "I am a Happy Man." In the book, Ed illustrated each ingredient with one of his paintings.

As you might guess, the decision to coauthor *Reinventing Masculinity* was fueled by Ed's need to create and contribute something of deep value. The central point of this effort was to create a book that could become a conduit for freeing other men (and women) to discover their soulful yearnings and express their many personal dimensions. And to that end, *Reinventing Masculinity: The Liberating Power of Compassion and Connection* is a creative act built upon the psychology of men.

Ed lives in the river town and arts community of Lambertville, New Jersey, with his wife, Marilee Adams, author and CEO of the Inquiry Institute, and their two dogs, Cloe and

Bodhi. Ed welcomes your thoughts, questions, and suggestions at info@ReinventingMasculinity.com.

Photo: Andria Lo

Ed Frauenheim   Ed Frauenheim has wrestled with what it means to be a man for four decades. In his personal and professional lives. As a young man, an adult, a father. As an observer of the best workplaces in the world. As cofounder of a group trying to reinvent organizations.

This book attempts to weave all these threads together.

The "man-rules" Ed grew up with weren't a good fit. Be strong? Ed was skinny. Dominate others? He lost his one fist fight in sixth grade. Just win, baby? He often froze during key moments of hockey, basketball, and soccer games.

The traditional male obsessions with winning, with brute strength, with becoming king of the corporate hill haunted Ed for much of his life. But through personal reflection, mindful practices, and plenty of help, he has come to redefine as worthy traits like emotional sensitivity, exuberance, and camaraderie. He's living a fuller life as a result—and hopes he's become a better husband and father to his two teens.

Ed's progress as a man owes partly to interviewing and learning about some of the most admirable men in business. Ed is an author who has written about organizations, leadership, and society for more than two decades. He currently serves as senior director of content at research and advisory firm Great Place to Work. Ed also cofounded the Teal Team, a small group aiming to help organizations evolve into more democratic, purpose-driven, soulful places.

Ed has cowritten three other books, including *A Great Place to Work for All: Better for Business, Better for People, Better for the World*. As a writer and public speaker, Ed has explored how our more-complex, interconnected economy is calling on men to break free of a narrow version of masculinity.

While a culture war rages in the mass media over what it means to be a man, Ed has contributed to a less-visible though vibrant conversation in the world of work. He has observed a growing consensus in the business world that men must shift from being rigid, cold, and isolated to flexible, warm, and connected. Ed has sought to bridge these conversations to show how men are reinventing masculinity at work.

Ed isn't done wrestling with what it means to be a man. But it's less a fight than a dance these days. And he hopes to help other men feel freer as they move through the world.

Also by Ed Frauenheim

Good Company
Business Success in the Worthiness Era
Laurie Bassi, Ed Frauenheim, and Dan McMurrer,
with Larry Costello

We've entered a new era in which good corporate behavior is no longer optional: it's the new imperative for success—and this book has the data to prove it. The authors' Good Company Index ranking of the Fortune 100 takes the belief in the bottom-line benefits of good behavior out of the realm of faith and into the realm of facts.

Print, hardcover, ISBN 978-1-60994-061-4
PDF ebook, ISBN 978-1-60994-062-1
ePub ebook, ISBN 978-1-60994-063-8

A Great Place to Work for All
**Better for Business, Better for People,
Better for the World**
Michael C. Bush, CEO, and the Great Place to Work
Research Team

Through inspiring stories and compelling research, the authors demonstrate that Great Places to Work for All benefit the individuals working there and contribute to a better global society—even as they outperform in the stock market and grow revenue three times faster than less-inclusive rivals. This is a call to lead so that organizations bring out the best in everyone.

Print, paperback, ISBN 978-1-5230-9508-7
PDF ebook, ISBN 978-1-5230-9509-4
ePub ebook, ISBN 978-1-5230-9510-0
Digital audio, ISBN 978-1-5230-9512-4

BK Berrett–Koehler Publishers, Inc.
www.bkconnection.com

800.929.2929